A Gen Xer's Guide to the Zombie Apocalypse

A How-To for the Seriously Unprepared

Joshua Thompson

Published by Gen Xer Guides

Printed in the United States of America

ISBN: 979-8-9941524-0-9

Imprint: Gen Xer Guides

First Edition

For information, contact: joshua@genexerguides.com

For everyone who is sick of the bullshit.

Contents

Part III: Rebuilding the World (Because Someone Has To, Apparently)

My Story & Why I Wrote This Book

I didn't write this to be a hero. I certainly didn't write it to build a personal brand. And God knows I didn't write it to start a conversation.

The idea for this book actually started where all great modern tragedies begin: a comment section. A Zoomer was online, confidently bashing Gen X, blaming us for the dumpster fire the Boomers started. She was way off base. We didn't break the world; we just learned to navigate the wreckage. I ended the debate by pointing out that when the zombie apocalypse hits, it will be up to Gen X to save the world and rebuild society, simply because we are the only generation equipped to do so.

That got me thinking. You see, I'm not just a grumpy observer. I have the receipts.

I spent a massive chunk of my life in the food service industry. It was awful, it was visceral, and it taught me everything I need to know about hungry, mindless hordes. In 2010, I escaped the kitchen and ran to academia. I picked up a BS in Psychology from Washington State, an MS in Experimental Psychology from Western Washington University, and an MBA in Business Analytics from the University of Tennessee Chattanooga.

On paper, I am a data nerd who works in public education systems with a few peer-reviewed publications and a TEDx Talk on political psychology. But in the context of the end of the world, that just means I am an expert in human behavior, persuasion, and logistics. I know how the mob thinks, I know why they panic, and I have the data to predict exactly how fast society will collapse.

I wrote this because I am tired.

For the last thirty years, our generation has been the something else in the demographic breakdown. We were the slackers in the 90s, the disaffected in the 2000s, and the forgotten ever since. We were the latchkey kids left to fend for ourselves with a house key on a shoelace and a terrifying lack of supervision. We were told our cynicism was a character flaw. We were told our apathy was a problem. We were told that our ability to sit in a room and stare at a ceiling for three hours was a sign of depression, not a survival skill.

They were wrong. As it turns out, we weren't slacking. We were waiting.

I wrote this book because when the world finally breaks—and it is *always* breaking—the two loudest generations in history are going to lose their minds. The Boomers are going to demand to speak to the apocalypse's manager. The Millennials and Gen Z are going to try to process the trauma of the horde while live-streaming their own panic.

And someone has to be the adult in the room.

I wrote this because I realized that the specific, weird, unsupervised trauma of a 1980s childhood wasn't neglect; it was boot camp. We learned to forage for food in a kitchen that contained nothing but condiments and stale crackers. We learned to fix broken technology by hitting it. We learned that if you get hurt and you don't die, you don't talk about it. We learned that the authorities are usually lying, incompetent, or both.

I wrote this manual so you would know how to siphon gas without swallowing it. I wrote it so you would know how to manage a group of survivors who are obsessed with consensus when they should be obsessed with survival. I wrote it because if I have to fix one more generator while someone lectures me about the ethics of fuel consumption, I am going to feed myself to the zombies.

But mostly, I wrote this as a love letter to the mediocre (society's label. Not mine). To the janitors, the fixers, the people in the back of the room who just want to get the job done and go home.

This isn't a manifesto for saving the world. The world is already gone. This is a guide to enduring what comes next with your sanity—and your record collection—intact.

So, read up. Learn how to be quiet. Learn how to be bored. Learn how to fix the damn pipe.

And then, please, leave me alone. I have a book to read.

You're welcome.

A Gen Xer's Guide to the Zombie Apocalypse

Part I
Our Origin Story (AKA: Why We're Not Already Dead)

EMERGENCY

COMMUNITY HUDDLE

3:00 PM SHARP

(BRING A SNACK TO SHARE)

Chapter 1
So, the World Ended.
You're Welcome

The Day the Noise Got Noisier

As it turns out, the end of the world wasn't a bang. It was a PTA meeting.

Someone—and I'd put money on the lady in the World's Best Mom sweatshirt who was now trying to laminate an Evacuation Routes flyer with a cold-press machine she'd liberated from the office—had insisted on a formal gathering. We'd found a flyer taped to the gym door, written in Comic Sans:

Emergency Community Huddle! 3:00 PM SHARP! (Bring a snack to share!)

The PA system was feeding back, a high-pitched whine that drilled directly into your skull. It was a sound I'd spent my entire adolescence learning to ignore, but here it was again, the official soundtrack to our extinction. We were in the gymnasium of a high school—a place that already smelled like floor wax, anxiety, and institutional-grade beef. The fluorescent lights hummed, casting a sickly, greenish glow that made everyone look, appropriately, half-dead.

Outside, the walking corpses were scratching at the steel doors. It was a faint, rhythmic scrape-drag, scrape-drag, like a thousand pieces of sandpaper being pulled across the wall. It was the only sound that mattered.

Inside, nobody was listening.

"If we don't form a sub-committee on resource allocation, we are inviting chaos!" a man in a golf shirt (Bob, probably) was shouting into the microphone, his voice echoing and distorting into a digital howl.

I was watching a perfect, real-time example of groupthink. The walking dead outside? That was the out-group. The meeting inside? That was the desperate, pathetic attempt to reinforce the in-group by creating the illusion of control. Bob wasn't making a plan; he was performing a social ritual. He was the tribe's shaman, dancing to ward off the storm, only his dance was a PowerPoint deck he was drawing on a whiteboard.

4

The first rule of the apocalypse: the most dangerous thing isn't the zombie. It's the person with the clipboard.

This was day four, and we hadn't come here for a plan. We'd come because we heard the vending machines were still working. But the meeting had been mandatory. The doors were locked. And now, as a zombie (who looked suspiciously like the Home Ec teacher) rhythmically slammed its head against the wired-glass window, the living—who were, somehow, infinitely worse—were trying to manage the situation.

In the corner, a guy in a full CrossFit kit was loudly critiquing the gym teacher's terrified attempt to barricade the door. "No, no, no, you gotta brace from the bottom! That's all leverage!" he yelled, not moving to help, just critiquing the form. "You're gonna lose your whole center of gravity!"

It wasn't panic. It wasn't fear. It was...annoyance. A profound, bone-deep, existential exasperation. The world had finally, finally pulled the plug, and these assholes were trying to put it on the agenda.

The Boomers and Robert's Rules of Zombie Management

At the front of the gym, Bob-in-the-Golf-Shirt had found an easel and a whiteboard. He was, I am not kidding, drawing an org chart.

"Okay, people, let's get organized!" he shouted, his voice cracking over the PA he refused to step away from. "We need to action this! I'm appointing Jim (a man cowering by the wrestling mats) as head of the Perimeter Security Steering Committee. We'll have a 7:00 AM daily stand-up."

This is what they do. They run things. They are the generation that was handed a functioning world and are baffled that this new, less functioning one isn't responding to their management style. They are trying to run the apocalypse.

Bob was now using the term zombie as if it were a quarterly loss. "We need to manage our Q4 undead-containment numbers, people! Let's circle back and action the perimeter item. What are the key deliverables for EOD?"

A woman with a perfect blonde helmet of hair, who looked like she'd been demanding to see a manager her entire life, was now demanding to see the manager of the apocalypse. "This is unacceptable," she was telling the cowering gym teacher. "I've been on hold with FEMA for twenty minutes. The customer service is just appalling. I want a refund."

A refund. For the apocalypse.

This was their entire response: a flurry of motions, agendas, and Robert's Rules of Order. They weren't doing anything; they were just scheduling the doing of it. They were genuinely offended that the zombies weren't respecting their property lines, and were, I overheard, discussing a strongly worded letter to the CDC. They were trying to apply 1980s corporate theory to a problem that was actively trying to eat them.

They're still trying to win the game that just got unplugged. They haven't realized that seniority doesn't stop a bite to the neck. They're still waiting to speak to the manager, not understanding that the manager just got eaten on the front lawn.

The Millennials and the Apocalypse as a Shared Trauma

The Boomers were trying to run the apocalypse. The Millennials were trying to feel it.

Over on the foul-smelling wrestling mats, a circle of them had formed, knees pulled to chests. This was, apparently, the designated safe space. They were processing. They were holding space for their feelings, which seemed to be numerous and loud.

"I just need to feel validated in my fear right now," a man with a beard bun was saying, his voice thick with the gravity of his own emotions. "I mean, why is this happening to *us*? We bought the avocado toast. We did the recycling. It's just...a lot."

It wasn't just processing; it was competitive processing. Who was the most traumatized? Whose narrative was the most valid? "I just feel like," another person added, "that my childhood fear of *Return*

6

of the Living Dead is really being centered right now, and I need to unpack that."

They were terrified, of course, but more than that, they seemed worried about the emotional labor of survival. They were trying to find an authentic post-apocalyptic experience. They were trying to find the hero's journey in the middle of a slaughter, but they were all stuck on the refusal of the call.

"I'm just not comfortable with the word looting," a woman in (now useless) yoga pants said. "It feels...problematic. Can we get a consensus on whether we're foraging or scavenging? Because looting implies a value judgment."

They were paralyzed by the need for 100% consensus. Before anyone could go look for food, they had to have a 45-minute discussion to ensure that the act of looking for food was equitable and didn't privilege the non-hungry. The result? Everyone was still hungry, but at least their feelings about it had been validated.

Someone else nodded, adding, "And, honestly? I feel like the zombies' lived experience isn't being centered here. What if they're just...misunderstood?"

I wanted to tell him that their lived experience was eating your face, but that would be emotional labor, and I was already exhausted.

They think the world is ending at them, a personal affront to their curated lives. They don't need a plan; they need a team, a therapist, and a trophy just for surviving the meeting. They're paralyzed, just sitting there on the mats, waiting for an authority figure—God, the government, a brand manager, someone—to finally show up and apologize.

Gen Z and the Curated Catastrophe

And then there was Gen Z. They weren't running the meeting, and they weren't processing in the circle. They were experiencing the apocalypse the only way they knew how: through their phones.

The phones were dead, of course. The grid was down, the network gone. It didn't matter. Muscle memory is a powerful thing.

Half a dozen of them were clustered near the bleachers, phones held up, live-streaming the committee meeting to an audience of zero. One of them was adding imaginary text to his imaginary video: "This whole vibe is giving...societal collapse," he muttered, narrating his own curated catastrophe.

Another was trying to get a selfie with the zombie-Home-Ec-teacher in the background, who was still smashing her face against the glass. "The juxtaposition is...everything," she muttered, tilting her chin. "It's giving...societal collapse but make it fashion." They weren't horrified by the end of the world; they were just worried that its aesthetic was cheugy.

And they were complaining. Not about the zombies, but about the accommodations. "Does anyone know if the cafeteria has non-GMO, gluten-free options? Because all I'm seeing in the vending machine is, like, poison."

The Millennial safe space on the wrestling mats? They'd already declared it a failure. "It's not an actual safe space," one of them announced to no one in particular. "Which is basically false advertising."

They were offended by the language, offended by the snacks, offended by the reality. "And honestly," another one added, "the survivor narrative is inherently ableist and reinforces a toxic grind culture."

"Can we not use the Z-slur?" a kid with green hair asked the terrified gym teacher. "It's an othering term. We prefer alternatively animated."

They're not in shock. They're just...annoyed. They're waiting for the world to conform to their needs, not the other way around. They've mistaken surviving for branding, and they're all vying to be the new apocalypse influencer.

And Then There's Us (The Whatever)

So, where were we in this three-ring circus of societal collapse?

We weren't at the podium. We weren't on the whiteboard. We weren't in the feeling circle.

We were in the back. Of course.

We were on the cold, metal bleachers, about three-quarters of the way up, near the emergency exit. We've always been near the exit. We've been sitting in the back of the class, the back of the bus, and the back of the pointless corporate meeting our entire lives. It's the only place to get a clear view of the whole, ridiculous stage.

And we were observing.

We weren't listening to Bob's Robert's Rules of Zombie Management, and we certainly weren't centering our feelings. We were running a different kind of triage. A quiet one.

We were inventorying the assets:

- That guy in the hiking boots? Asset. He's quiet, but he's re-laced his boots twice. He's ready to move.
- The woman who looks like a high school vice-principal and hasn't stopped glaring? Asset. She's got a keychain with 30 keys on it. She's a gatekeeper in the literal sense.
- The CrossFit guy? Liability. All show, no go. He'll pull a hamstring trying to impress everyone and then need all the good bandages.
- The quiet lunch lady who was methodically sharpening a spatula on the concrete floor? Hard asset. She's already accepted the new reality and is weaponizing her environment.
- The beard-bun guy who is literally shaking? Soon-to-be-food.
- The Gen Z kid complaining about the snacks? Surprisingly, an asset. He's a forager by nature. He knows where all the hidden stashes are. You just have to tune out the complaining.

We were noting the structural weaknesses. This gymnasium? A fucking death trap. Too many single-pane glass doors. That PA system? A dinner bell. The acoustics? A nightmare.

And we were silently, almost unconsciously, calculating the real resources. I'd been counting the spirals in the snack-bar vending

9

machine by the entrance. Thirteen rows, maybe ten items per row. At least forty of those items were snack-bar-sized bags of Doritos. Pure sodium and air. 150 calories a bag. Useless, but good for morale. The Snickers? 250 calories, fat, sugar, peanuts. A decent short-term fuel. But the real prize, in the back, E-7? Big Texas cinnamon rolls. 400+ calories of pure, processed, shelf-stable glucose. That wasn't a snack; that was emergency-room-level go fuel. That was the get-you-over-the-wall energy. I'd already mentally cataloged three of them. Three Big Texas rolls. 1,200 calories. That's 48 hours of operational energy if I don't move much. The CrossFit guy will burn through that in 20 minutes of dynamic stretching. They are wasted on him. They are mine.

In fact, that's the only reason we were here. We didn't come for the meeting. We came to see if the little green light on the vending machine was still on.

And as we sat there, listening to the Boomer's agenda, the Millennial's trauma, and the Zoomer's vibe check, it happened. A profound, collective, non-verbal realization passed between those of us on the bleachers.

It was the great Gen X Shrug Moment.

"Oh. Shit."

It was the feeling of being 13 years old, home alone, and hearing a crash from the kitchen. This was just 1987 all over again. It was the feeling of walking home, finding the front door accidentally locked, and realizing your parents were at a conference and had forgotten you. You'd have to use a credit card (or, in this case, a cafeteria butter knife) to jimmy the lock, find your 6-year-old brother, and then deal with whatever small-to-medium-sized disaster he had created... usually involving the toaster, a G.I. Joe, and a fire extinguisher.

The world has become one giant, unsupervised Saturday afternoon, and the house is on fire.

This isn't a shock to us. It's just...an inconvenience. We've been the clean-up crew our entire lives. We were the generation sandwiched between Boomer messes and Millennial expectations. We've been quietly fixing the server, translating the HR policy, and doing the actual work while they took the credit or processed their feelings about the workload. This? This is just the final, biggest mess they've left for us to clean up.

Our apathy? That's just high-level energy conservation. We've been saving our fucks to give for a real crisis, and well, here it is. Our cynicism? That's just pattern recognition. We *knew* the system was a house of cards. We're just the only ones not surprised to see it fall. Our slacker reputation? That was just us, waiting. Waiting for everyone else to finally shut up so we could get this over with.

The Mission Statement: You're Welcome.

So, fine. We'll save the world. But we're doing it our way.

And because we're the only ones who know how to do anything, we're also going to write the fucking manual. This is it. You're holding it. Consider this the official Welcome to the Apocalypse packet that the Boomer committee was too busy laminating to actually write.

Let's be clear about what this is. This is not a self-help book. This is not a *Chicken Soup for the Apathetic Soul*. This is not a journal with prompts about how the horde makes you feel. We are not going to inspire you. We are not thought leaders, and we are not your life coaches.

This is a manual. This is the IKEA instruction booklet for rebuilding society, written with the appropriate, mandatory level of exasperation. It's got confusing diagrams, half the steps are missing, and you're pretty sure the little Allen wrench it came with is a cosmic joke. But unlike that MALM dresser, this thing has to be built, and it has to work, or you're all going to die.

This book is not a place for your feelings. It's not a validation journal. It is, most pointedly, not a committee meeting. It is a one-way transmission of information. We're not getting consensus on this. We're not circling back to ideate. This is the plan. It's done.

Our promise is simple: We're not going to hold your hand. We're going to give you practical, snarky, battle-tested advice on how to survive when everyone else is making it all about them. We're going to teach you how to fix a generator, how to siphon gas, how to manage the Millennial who needs to process the zombie breach, and how to tell the Boomer who wants to form a sub-committee to go fuck himself (politely, of course; we're passive-aggressive, not monsters).

Why us? Why Gen X?

Because we're the only ones prepared for this. We were raised on a steady diet of benign neglect, broken technology, and spectacularly low expectations. The Boomers were told they were special. The Millennials were told they were special. We were just... told to go play outside and not come back until the streetlights came on.

We are the last generation to remember life before the internet. When the Cloud collapses, we're the only ones who can read a paper map, use a payphone, or hotwire a 1992 Honda Civic. We're the only ones who know how to be bored—who can stand watch for eight hours without having a psychotic break because our phone isn't feeding us content. A Millennial's brain chemistry will short-circuit after 20 minutes. A Zoomer will literally vibrate apart. Us? We can sit on a roof for eight hours, stare at a wall, and call it Tuesday.

We can fix a VCR, which means we understand input/output and troubleshooting with our hands. We can make a mixtape, which means we understand pacing, narrative, and—most critically— resource management (you only had 90 minutes, dammit, and you had to commit).

They call it neglect. We call it unsupervised field research. We didn't get participation trophies, so we're not paralyzed when we don't get one for surviving. We weren't told we were special, so we don't have a crisis of self-worth when the universe doesn't seem to care about our feelings. Our cynicism isn't a mood; it's a highly developed, predictive threat-assessment model. We just call it seeing things. And we've been seeing things for 30 years.

This apocalypse? This is our fucking latchkey privilege. The world is just a bigger, emptier house with the parents gone for good. Except this time, the stranger danger is real, and the call is definitely coming from inside the house.

So, let's get this over with. The world you knew is gone.

Chapter 2
The Latchkey Privilege: An Origin Story

The Click, The Silence, and The School of Fend for Yourself

Do you remember the sound of a 1980s afternoon?

It wasn't a ping or a vibration. It was a jingle. The sound of a single, brassy house key, its edges worn smooth, rattling on a dirty shoelace loop or inside a gritty, Velcro-flapped wallet. It was the scratch-scratch-jiggle of that key finding the deadbolt.

Then, the thwack of the aluminum screen door hitting the frame, followed by the heavy, definitive click of the deadbolt sliding home.

And then...silence.

Not a scary silence. Not an oh-my-god-I'm-all-alone silence. Just...the baseline, 3:30 PM silence of an empty house. The hum of the fridge. The muffled sound of *General Hospital* from the neighbor's house. The air in that house had a specific smell: floor wax, old carpet, the faint, sweet-and-sour tang of a half-empty box of Apple Jacks, and the dusty, hot-plastic smell of the 27-inch Zenith TV that was, at this very moment, our god.

This was the immediate, total, and glorious lack of supervision.

This wasn't neglect. This was the latchkey privilege.

We were given a four-hour window, five days a week, to become absolute masters of our own small, shag-carpeted domains. We were our own bosses, our own chefs, and our own first responders. The rules were simple, unwritten, and absolute:

1. Don't burn it down.

2. Don't bleed on the good couch (we'll get to that).

3. If you eat it, you are responsible for the evidence.

4. Be at the kitchen table, homework open, by 5:45 PM for the good ki' performance art.

The apocalypse experts have a term for this: operating without support.

We just called it Tuesday.

16

The other generations see this new, empty, terrifying world and they panic. They're waiting for the adults to get home and tell them what to do. We just see a bigger house with the parents gone for good.

The fridge could wait. The first act was always the TV. Clicking the heavy, resistant knob...click-click-click...past the PBS snooze-fest, past the soaps, landing on the forbidden paradise: Channel 32. MTV. "Welcome to the Jungle" hitting the air in a silent house wasn't just music; it was a conquest.

Foraging (AKA: Inventing Meals from Despair and Condiments)

The latchkey privilege came with its first and most important daily challenge: The 3:45 PM famine.

Our parents, champions of benign neglect, left us with a hostile food landscape. The kitchen was a culinary wasteland of canned goods (mostly creamed corn), questionable leftovers sealed in a fogged-up Tupperware, and the dusty end-of-bag crumbs from a box of stale cereal. We were expected to fend for ourselves. And fend, we did.

We were the original Iron Chefs of processed food. Our secret ingredient was always despair (and probably ketchup). We were culinary Rube Goldbergs, masters of creating a meal from the unlikeliest of parts.

Welcome to the Latchkey Hall of Fame:

The Microwave-Saddened Hot Dog: You learned that a single, lonely hot dog (no bun, obviously) could be sliced, microwaved until it curled into a sad, pink C, and then eaten with a dip made of mustard and grape jelly. Why? Because they were both *in the door*. It was sweet and savory. We were pioneers.

The Sadness Grilled Cheese: You learned that two slices of Wonder Bread, a Kraft Single (still in its plastic, you'd just peel the melted parts off), and 45 seconds in the microwave produced a grilled cheese that was 90% sadness and 10% sustenance.

The Cereal Dust Sludge: The act of pouring the last, pulverized sugar-dust from three different boxes of Cap'n Crunch, Froot Loops, and Cookie Crisp into one bowl, adding just enough milk to create a

17

diabetic-coma-inducing sludge. It was 90% sugar, 10% regret, and 100% fuel.

The Pillsbury Doughboy Improv: Discovering that a can of Pillsbury crescent rolls could be unrolled, wrapped around *anything*—a hot dog, a Fun Size Snickers, a lump of cheddar—baked at 350°F, and be considered gourmet.

The Archaeological Dig: The bravery required to excavate the depths of a chest freezer, past the frost-fur, to unearth a Salisbury Steak TV dinner from 1984. It was a game of 'Is this still food?' The answer was always '...probably.'

We didn't just understand the five-second rule; we viewed it as a ridiculously conservative guideline. It was more of a five-minute, check-for-hair, and wipe-it-on-your-jeans protocol.

And now, this is called looting.

While the other survivors are paralyzed in a ransacked Piggly Wiggly, having a full-blown existential crisis, we see a goldmine. I watched a Millennial in the international aisle, holding two jars of artisanal salsa, literally shaking. "I just don't know which one has a more authentic narrative!" he cried. In the next aisle, a Zoomer was trying to scan a can of Libby's pumpkin filling with his dead phone. "I just need to know if the brand is, like, problematic before I eat it."

We are not shoppers. We are scroungers.

They see a warm, half-flat 2-liter of Shasta and are literally disgusted. We see hydration and 300 sugar calories. They see a bag of stale Fritos. We see a viable carb, and also, kindling. They see a dented, labelless can and worry about botulism. We just shrug, grab it, and figure we'll find out what it is later. We are the masters of the dented can economy.

We don't need a fucking recipe. We don't need an organic label. We don't need consensus on the ethics of taking the last can of SpaghettiOs. We need calories. And we have a Ph.D. in turning crap into calories.

Crisis Management (AKA: Don't. Bleed. On. The. Couch.)

The second, inevitable lesson of the latchkey privilege was that unsupervised freedom has consequences. And those consequences hurt.

We were the last generation of bareheaded bike riders. We flew over handlebars, ate gravel, and learned about physics from a curbstone. We were the budding chemists who discovered that mixing Windex and Clorox in the bathroom sink was a bad idea.

We all built the ramp. A single, warped piece of plywood propped on a cinder block, set at the end of a driveway. It was a perfect launchpad to glory, which usually meant the emergency room. My Huffy banana-seat hit the ramp, I achieved three seconds of glorious air, and then 45 pounds of steel and 70 pounds of stupid came down on a sidewalk. The gravel wasn't just eaten; it was embedded in my knee, and the blood was...well, it was leaking aggressively.

When these minor disasters struck, there was no adult to run to. There was no one to process the trauma with. There was only... the triage. We learned, instinctively, to run the Triage of Parental Consequences. It was a simple, three-point checklist:

1. Am I dying? (e.g., Is the blood squirting? Is the bone outside the skin?) The answer was almost always 'No.'

2. Can I fix this myself? The answer was almost always 'Probably.'

3. Will they know?

This was the most important question. "Will they know" translated to "Will I get in trouble for this?" And the answer had to be 'No.'

This is why we became radical self-rescuers. We didn't patch our wounds to get better; we patched them to hide the evidence. We became masters of the 1980s bathroom field-op.

You're in the bathroom, door locked. The air smells of Brylcreem and Aqua Net. You open the medicine cabinet.

Step 1: Grab the brown plastic bottle of hydrogen peroxide. You pour it on, not because it works (it doesn't), but because the bubbling meant it was doing something.

Step 2: The Bandage Fail. You grab a wad of single-ply toilet paper, which instantly disintegrates and becomes part of the wound. This is a disaster. You upgrade: a paper towel held in place with Scotch tape (which falls off in 30 seconds).

Step 3: The Pro Move. You find a Maxi-Pad from under the sink, slap it on the wound, and secure it with three wraps of your dad's gray-green duct tape. It was a perfect, absurd, and completely effective pressure bandage.

This is radical self-reliance. It was beaten into us by circumstance.

And now, in the apocalypse, we are our own first responders because we've always been. A zombie has torn a gash in the CrossFit guy's arm. The Millennials are holding space for his pain journey. The Boomers are forming a committee on medical supplies. We just sigh, grab the duct tape and a cleanish T-shirt, and fix it.

We're not waiting for FEMA. We're not waiting for the CDC. We're not waiting for Mom. The other survivors are paralyzed, waiting for the authorities to save them. We just see the zombie as a bigger, uglier version of that bike wreck. We don't panic. We just...fix it. And we try not to bleed on the couch, because that's a bitch to clean up.

Situational Awareness (AKA: The 5:30 PM Parent-Detector)

This was the final, and most advanced, latchkey skill. It was a primal sense we all developed, a kind of low-grade, constant paranoia that we just called the afternoon.

It was the 5:30 PM parent-detector.

You'd be deep in a forbidden activity—watching MTV instead of doing homework, three-quarters of the way through a box of Ho Hos, trying to see the good channel on the scrambled cable box—and you'd feel it. A shift in the air. A vibration.

It was the precise, gut-level sense of the garage door opener rattling in its track. The distant sound of tires crunching on the driveway gravel. The click of a key in the front door that was 30 minutes too early.

It was threat level midnight.

What followed was the 90-second panic-clean. It was an art form, a symphony of frantic, silent motion. A drill we ran daily.

Phase 1: The Sound. The faintest rumble of the garage door.

Phase 2: Threat Assessment. A frantic glance at the clock. 5:32 PM. They're on time. Crap.

Phase 3: Evidence Elimination. This was the sprint. The six Pudding Pop wrappers shoved deep into the bottom of the kitchen trash. The soda can rinsed and hidden. The *Tiger Beat* magazine kicked under the couch.

Phase 4: Staging. Click the TV off. Frantically rub the static off the screen with your sleeve (the hot screen was a dead giveaway). Grab a textbook. Open it to a random page.

Phase 5: The performance. A bored, "Oh. Hi. You're home early," as the door opens.

Mission accomplished. That, right there, is high-level threat assessment. We were bug-out experts before we could drive.

Our ears are tuned for the-sound-that-doesn't-belong. The others? They're sound generators. The Boomer is trying to call a meeting in the open street. The Millennial is trying to build community by talking...loudly. The Zoomer has found a solar-powered speaker and is curating the apocalypse vibe with a playlist.

We're the only ones who hear the scrape-drag from two blocks away, because we're the only ones who know how to shut the fuck up. We instinctively know the difference between the foot-drag of a zombie and the footstep of a looter. We know when to hide, when to be quiet, and when to look busy (i.e., like you belong there).

While everyone else is arguing in the middle of a ransacked street, we've already heard the sound of a window breaking three blocks away... and we've already disappeared.

The Psychological Armor of the Ignored

But the latchkey privilege wasn't just about the practical skills. It was the emotional conditioning. It was the psychological armor we built, layer by layer, every single afternoon.

We learned to be alone without being lonely.

This is a concept that is, frankly, incomprehensible to the other generations. They confuse being alone with being in active, mortal danger. The Zoomers require constant connection, validation, and feedback. The Millennials need a squad, a consensus, and a community vibe. They were raised in a world of constant, curated social interaction. Being left alone is a punishment or a crisis.

For us, it was the goal.

We learned to self-soothe. We didn't have anyone to hold space for our B-minus-on-a-test trauma. We didn't have a community to process our feelings with when we got cut from the team. We just... went to our rooms, put on a mixtape (the one that started with 'How Soon Is Now?'), and marinated in our own acceptable, low-grade angst until it passed. We didn't have a therapist; we had The Cure. We didn't have validation; we had R.E.M. We learned to live inside our own heads, to find our own center without a fucking yoga mat or a group-therapy session.

This emotional self-sufficiency is our single greatest superpower. We are masters of boredom. The others are addicted to external stimuli; their brains are content junkies going through withdrawal. We marinated in no-content. Our content was the water stains on the ceiling, the lyrics on a cassette-tape insert, the plot of a *Choose Your Own Adventure* book. We learned to live inside our own heads, and as it turns. out, our heads are a pretty fucking useful place to be.

In the apocalypse, we can stand watch for 12 hours without going insane. We don't need a team-building exercise or a community check-in to feel secure. We aren't going to have a full-blown existential crisis because the Wi-Fi is down and we can't process our day.

We've been un-processed our whole lives. Our baseline is already "the world is vaguely disappointing and no one is here to help."

This? This isn't a catastrophe. It's just a change of scenery.

The World Is Our Empty House Now

So, there it is. The latchkey privilege. It was our secret, unsupervised, slightly-sad-but-mostly-awesome training ground.

The generational divide in the apocalypse is simple. The Boomers are panicked because, for the first time in their lives, no one is in charge of them, and they've forgotten how to function without a hierarchy to lead (or complain to). The younger generations are panicked because no one is taking care of them; the entire support structure of validation, safety, and curated experience has been ripped away.

And us? We're...fine.

We're fine because we've always been in this in-between space. We're the forgotten middle children, the kids who raised themselves. And as it turns out, we're the only ones who remember how.

The apocalypse didn't break us. It didn't traumatize us. It just finally gave us a problem big enough to match our weird, duct-taped, self-reliant skill set.

Of course, surviving the empty house was one thing. Surviving the soundtrack was another. All that self-soothing we did? It came with a side of profound, existential dread that we've been nursing for thirty years.

And that dread... that's our next superpower. Let's call it the cynicism advantage.

Chapter 3
The Soundtrack to Our Apathy: How to Not Freak Out When Your Neighbor Is Eating the Mailman

The "Oh, This" Moment

The gymnasium meeting was a farce, but the street-level view was the real deal. This was the first, unfiltered moment of chaos. The sirens had given up, their single, looped wails just blending into a background of distant screaming and the whoomp of a car on fire.

And, of course, there was Gary, our neighbor from 728, who was, at that very moment, gnawing on the mailman.

The generational reactions were...predictable.

"This is UNACCEPTABLE!" a Boomer screamed from his porch, actually shaking his fist. "I'm calling the police! This is a complete failure of leadership!" He was genuinely outraged, as if the zombies were a rival company that had just violated an NDA.

From a window above, a Millennial was hyperventilating into a dead phone. "I'm literally shaking right now! This is...this is so traumatizing! I can't even...I can't process this!"

And us? We were just...watching.

I was on my porch. I didn't scream. I didn't run. I just...stopped. I lowered my coffee mug, which had gone cold. I put my hand on the door frame. And I just watched for a second. It was...grotesque. It was fascinating. It was inevitable. My first concrete thought wasn't "Oh my god!" It was, "Huh. So that's what that looks like. He's really committing to it. Good for Gary, I guess. He never did like that mailman. I wonder if this means the Amazon package isn't coming."

We took a long, slow exhale. This wasn't panic. This wasn't shock. It was a deep, profound, bone weary sense of recognition.

"Oh," we thought, collectively. "This."

We're not freaking out because we've been waiting for this. Our entire adolescence was a 24/7 existential-dread-delivery-system. Our childhood was a fear-of-the-week club. We were the duck and cover generation's kids, and they passed the paranoia on to us, only now it was *real*.

We were promised nuclear war. We sat in classrooms in 1983 watching *The Day After* on a rolling AV cart, a film so traumatizing

26

it was basically state-sanctioned child abuse. We went to bed that night knowing, with absolute certainty, that we would be vaporized in our sleep by a Soviet SS-18.

We were promised acid rain. We were told not to drink the rain. The fucking rain. We were told the ozone layer was gone and the sun was going to microwave us. We saw *WarGames* and knew a computer was going to kill us all. We saw *The Terminator* and knew a robot was going to kill us all. We saw *Red Dawn* and knew the Russians were going to kill us all.

This? A zombie? It's almost quaint. It's analog. You can see it. You can hit it with a shovel. Honestly, it's a relief. The world ending isn't news to us. It's just...finally getting around to it.

The Slacker as Strategic Energy Conservationist

This recognition is why they called us slackers. It's the label the Boomers slapped on us when they saw us refusing to participate in their rah-rah, go-go, greed is good '80s fantasy. We were the apathetic generation, the slackers, because we wouldn't play.

But it was never about being lazy. It was about an instinctive, gut-level refusal to waste energy on things that didn't matter. Our entire lives, we've had a finely tuned bullshit-detector for performative nonsense.

The Bullshit We Refused (Pre-Apocalypse):

- Corporate rah-rah culture and mandatory team building exercises. (No, I am not going to do a trust fall with Dave from accounting. I don't trust Dave.)

- Wacky Tie Day.

- Company picnics on a Saturday. That's not a picnic, that's a hostage situation.

- Wearing flair to prove our enthusiasm.

- Pointless meetings that could have been an email (or, better yet, nothing).

27

- Performative enthusiasm for a brand, a boss, or a quarterly projection.

- Chasing the Joneses in a game we knew was rigged.

We saw it all as a massive, exhausting waste of time. So, we'd show up, do the actual work, and go home. They called it slacking. We called it efficiency.

And now, in the post-apocalypse, the bullshit has changed, but our refusal remains the same.

The Bullshit We Refuse (Post-Apocalypse):

- Arguing about who's in charge when the real problem is the broken fence.

- Group processing sessions about how the horde makes us feel.

- Debating the ethics of looting versus foraging while we're actively starving.

- Any...*any*...activity that isn't directly related to calories, shelter, or not-being-eaten.

This isn't apathy. It's an emotional triage tool. We don't freak out because our brains, conditioned by decades of low-grade dread, don't let us. We automatically triage emotional data.

Let's take the neighbor-eating-mailman scenario. The other generations' entire emotional and intellectual operating system crashes. Their triage is a one-step loop: "OH MY GOD!"

Our triage, honed by years of practice, is just...different. It runs in the background, like a good piece of anti-virus software. We call it the Gen X triage.

Let's run the scenario. The Boomer is on the phone to...who? The President? He's creating noise and wasting energy. The Millennial is having a panic attack, using resources (air, sound, someone else's time to calm them down). What are we doing? We're running the triage:

1. Threat: High. (Zombie.)

2. Proximity: 50 yards. (Medium.)

3. My Problem? Not...yet. He's occupied. Mailman's a goner.

4. Action: Lock the front door. Move to the back of the house. Check the deadbolts on all the doors. Get the crowbar from the garage.

This entire process takes 1.5 seconds. It's not a panic; it's a workflow We've just processed an 'OH MY GOD' event, given it a low-priority flag in the queue, and moved it to the to-do list. We'll get to it after coffee. That is the advantage. We don't let the event become an emotional catastrophe. We just see it as a new problem to be solved—or, in this case, a new problem to be ignored until it's at the door.

The Psychology of the Shrug (The Gen X Communication Toolkit)

That firewall isn't just internal. It has an external interface. Our apathy is backed up by a non-verbal communication toolkit that we've spent a lifetime perfecting.

This toolkit is now our most powerful survival tool, not for the zombies, but for dealing with the other survivors. It's our primary way of managing the emotional escalations of everyone else without burning a single unnecessary calorie.

Here is your arsenal:

1. The Shrug

- **Pre-Apocalypse:** "I don't know," "I don't care," or "Whatever." A simple, passive statement of neutrality or ignorance.

- **Post-Apocalypse:** "I am not participating in your hysterical escalation. This is not my problem to solve, and I refuse to let it become mine."

- **Use:** This is your primary defense against Millennial panic. When Chad runs up to you, vibrating with anxiety, and asks,

"Oh my god, what are we going to do? What's the plan?"—you just give him the shrug. It is a conversation ender. It's a nonverbal brick wall. It immediately deflates their panic by giving it nothing to push against. It forces them to either calm down or go find their own answer. It is a masterpiece of energy conservation.

2. The Eyeroll

- **Pre-Apocalypse:** "You've got to be kidding me." A reaction to a bad pun, a pointless directive from a boss, or an annoying commercial.

- **Post-Apocalypse:** "That is the single stupidest survival idea I have ever heard, and it is going to get us all killed."

- **Use:** This is your silent veto. When Bob the Boomer stands up at the gymnasium meeting and says, "We need to form a committee to elect a leader," and you're in the back by the exit, you just deploy the eyeroll. It's a binding, silent vote of no. It's a signal to the other sane people in the room that the person talking is an idiot. It's how you build a silent consensus of "this is bullshit" without ever having to say a word.

3. The Silent Stare

- **Pre-Apocalypse:** The look you gave your teacher after they asked a really stupid question.

- **Post-Apocalypse:** "I am waiting for you to finish your emotional tantrum so the adults can talk."

- **Use:** This is not an angry stare. Just...a blank one. The "you-are-a-talking-lump-of-stupid-and-I-am-just-waiting-for-you-to-stop" stare. It's what you give the Zoomer who's complaining that the vibe in the shelter is toxic. You don't argue. You just...stare. It's a psychological mute button.

4. The Sigh (The Exasperated Hiss)

- **Pre-Apocalypse:** "This meeting is pointless, and I want to go home."

- **Post-Apocalypse:** "Fine. You're all idiots. I'll do it myself."

- **Use:** This is the nuclear option. This is the sound of Gen X finally accepting the burden. This is the sound that precedes us just... getting up.

- **The Scene:** The generator is out. The Generator Task Force (four Boomers, three Millennials) has been ideating on a solution for *two hours*. They're drawing process-flow diagrams on a whiteboard. You're in the corner, trying to re-read a 1997 copy of *Wired*. Finally, you can't take it. You deploy the sigh. It's not a sad sigh. It's a "fuck-me-I-guess-I-have-to-do-this" sigh. You get up. You walk past the committee. You don't make eye contact. You grab the toolbox. You kick the generator. You pop the cover. The spark plug wire is loose. You jam it back on. You pull the cord. *VVRROOOM*. The lights flicker on. You don't look at them. You don't wait for a thank you. You just go back to your magazine. You've just saved them all, and you're pissed about it. That is the Gen X experience.

This toolkit isn't just snark for snark's sake. It's a critical boundary-setting mechanism. It's how we avoid the emotional labor (a term we would literally never use, but the concept is painfully real) of managing everyone else's feelings. We are not your therapists. We are not your life coach. We are not your parents, your boss, or your HR department. We're just trying to not get bitten, and we refuse to get eaten just because we were holding space for someone else's panic attack.

Cynicism Is Just Realism in a Flannel Shirt

It all ties together. That soundtrack we grew up with—the punk, the new wave, the grunge—wasn't just music. It was a prophecy. It was the "No Future" of the Sex Pistols. It was the "I'm so happy 'cuz today I found my friends, they're in my head" of Nirvana. It was the "world is a vampire" of Smashing Pumpkins.

It was the instruction manual for a life spent feeling disaffected and alienated. We didn't just listen to songs about the world being a sham; we marinated in them. We took notes.

That's the core insight. The other generations are in a state of profound, hysterical shock because the world they believed in has just collapsed. The Boomers are watching their order burn. The Millennials and Zoomers are watching their concepts of fairness, validation, and progress get eaten with the mailman. They are horrified because the system they trusted, or at least tried to engage with, has been revealed as a complete lie.

Our advantage? We never believed in it in the first place.

We've always known the adults were full of it. We were always the kid in the John Hughes movie, staring out the window, fully aware that the principal, the parents, and the popular kids were all running a scam. We were just waiting for the credits to roll.

We *are* the "Breakfast Club," 30 years later We're the Brat Pack, and we've realized the real enemy wasn't Principal Vernon. It was the entire fucking system... And now that system is gone. The school's been overrun, and it turns out the Brat Pack is the only group of specialists who can actually run the place. And Bender is the only one who knows how to pick a lock, Claire is the only one who can trade for supplies, Brian is the only one who can rig the generator, Allison is the only one who's been foraging this whole time, and Andrew is the only one strong enough to hold the door.

We're not slackers. We're specialists.

The world didn't end. It just finally started making sense. The existential dread we've been nursing since 1991 wasn't a bug; it was a feature. It was the background process that's been preparing us for this all along. We're not panicked. We're not even surprised.

We're just...annoyed that it's going to be this loud.

Of course, a good attitude is one thing. But when the lights go out for good, you can't brood your way to fresh water. You need skills. You need the analog advantage.

Chapter 4
The Analog Advantage: Surviving When the Cloud Collapses

The No Service Apocalypse

It was inevitable. We'd been running on patchy, ghost-in-the-machine service for a week. Then, on a Tuesday, the last bar of LTE flickered, held on for a stubborn, digital second, and was gone. The satellites went dark. The cellular network died. The cloud—that magical, invisible place where everyone stored their entire personality—evaporated.

The sound was immediate. A chorus of rising, panicked disbelief.

"Does anyone have a signal?" "It's just spinning! I've rebooted it twice!" "My Google Map just went blank! It's just...gray! How do we get to the Costco?"

Then, the truly terrified whimper from a Millennial in the corner: "My...my survival-plan-dot-doc was on the cloud! The whole plan! It's...gone!"

It wasn't just the map. It was *everything*. "My 'how-to-tie-a-tourniquet' video was bookmarked!" a Zoomer wailed. "I didn't even download it!" The Millennial who lost his survival-plan-dot-doc was now rocking back and forth. "It had links," he whimpered. "It had all the links. And...and my curated End of the World playlist on Spotify. How are we supposed to...vibe?"

In the next room, I watched a guy—full prepper gear, tactical beard, the works—staring at a pile of scavenged canned goods. He had his dead phone in his hand. "I...I can't log my calories," he said, his voice a quiet horror. "My Fitbit app is offline. I don't...I don't know my macros." He was genuinely going to starve to death because an app couldn't tell him it was okay to eat the 190-calorie Chef Boyardee ravioli.

We were in the corner, checking our own phone. A five-year-old, cracked-screen special that was already obsolete before the world ended. We saw the No Service icon. We sighed. It was an annoyed sigh, sure—no more Words with Friends to kill the downtime. But it wasn't a catastrophe. We put the phone back in our pocket.

The other generations lost their brains when the cloud collapsed. We just lost a convenience. We're the last generation that was digitally bilingual—we grew up in the old world and learned the new one. And when the digital language went extinct overnight, we were the only ones left who were still fluent in analog.

You Are Here — The Lost Art of Knowing Where the Fuck You Are

Remember the family road trip? Remember the glove compartment, stuffed so full it would barely close? You'd pry it open and out would fall a five-inch-thick, spiral-bound Rand McNally atlas, smelling of stale coffee, paper, and Armor All.

This was our navigation. A book. We'd watch from the back seat as Mom tried to navigate by holding the map upside down while Dad refused to ask for directions, his knuckles white on the steering wheel. "The map says turn," she'd hiss. "There's a lake here, Frank!"

We learned through osmosis. We learned what scale means (one inch = 20 miles). We learned that the red lines are interstates, the little black-and-white shields are US Highways, and the thin, squiggly blue lines are the back roads that might have a gas station or might just have a very angry dog. We know that the sun generally rises in the east and sets in the west, a low-tech feature that still, miraculously, works.

The Scene: We're in a busted-up van at a crossroads. "We must stay on the Interstate!" Bob the Boomer is shouting. "It's the main route! It's the fastest! All leadership agrees!" "But...Google always said to take the interstate..." a Millennial adds, staring at his blank phone as if it betrayed him.

We just deploy the sigh. We get out, pop the hood of the van (it's covered in guts), and unfold the paper atlas.

"Bob, the interstate is a 200-mile-long, gridlocked parking lot. It's a death trap. There are no exits. You're a sitting duck. Google's dead. Look." I point with a greasy finger. "This red line? That's the interstate. This thin blue line? This is a state highway. It's slower. It also goes through twenty small towns. Which means twenty chances for gas, twenty pharmacies, twenty grocery stores. And it has fifty exit points. We're not taking the fastest route. We're taking the smartest one. We're going this way."

I get back in the van, which is somewhere in Ohio. I look at the sun. It's high, but that way. "It's about 2 PM," I say to no one. "That means that way is West. This road is running North-South. We need to go North. Let's go."

While the others are staring at a blank, gray screen, frantically rebooting, waiting for a little blue dot to save them, we're navigating

Rube Goldberg Repair — The Fix-It Gene

Remember the specific, plastic-sounding thwack of hitting the side of the NES to make it work? Remember blowing into the cartridge, a magical, dusty breath that resurrected Mario? Remember using a pencil to painstakingly rewind a cassette tape because the rewind button on your Walkman would drain the batteries in ten seconds?

Our technology was mechanical. It was understandable. It wasn't a sealed, magic black box. If it broke, you could open it up (voiding a warranty we never cared about) and see the problem—a snapped rubber belt, a loose gear, a dirty contact on a circuit board. This gave us the fix-it gene. It was a methodology built on duct tape, WD-40, and the "jiggle-it-till-it-works" protocol. It was ugly. It was imprecise. But it worked.

The Scene: Day 12. The generator sputters and dies. The lights go out. Immediate panic. "Dammit!" Bob yells. "Who has the manual? We need the 1-800 number!" "I'm Googling generator repair!...Oh. Right," says the Millennial. "This is so problematic," the Zoomer mutters. "It's using fossil fuels. Maybe this is a sign..."

I just deploy the sigh. I grab a single wrench and a flashlight. "It's the spark plug, you idiots. It's always the spark plug." I go out. I pop the cover. I unscrew the plug. It's black with carbon. I scrape it clean with my pocket knife. I wipe it on my jeans. I screw it back in. I jam the wire back on. I pull the cord. VVRROOOM. The lights flicker on. I walk back in, past the stunned committee. "Someone make coffee. Now."

The younger generations are app dependent. They're staring at a dead Prius wondering why the start button isn't responding, as if it needs a software update. We are tool dependent. We know how to siphon gas.

We found a parking lot full of dead cars. A fuel goldmine. The others were just...staring at them. "How do we get it out?" Chad asked. I just sighed, grabbed a three-foot section of garden hose, and walked to a '92 Honda Civic. "Watch," I said. I fed the hose in. "Now, you gotta suck." "You're gonna drink it?!" "No, you moron. You suck, you spit. You don't swallow. God, did your parents teach you nothing?" I gave a short, hard pull... got a faceful of gasoline... spit. And out it came. "Get the can."

Accessing the Meat-Cloud — Finding Info Without a Search Bar

Remember the smell of the Encyclopedia Britannica? That specific, dusty-sweet smell of old paper, ink, and binding glue? Remember the card catalog at the library, that giant wooden altar to the Dewey Decimal System?

We had to remember things. Phone numbers. Addresses. How to get to a friend's house. Our brains weren't just processors; they were hard drives. We didn't just ask the internet. We had to look. We learned how to use an index. We mastered the art of skimming. We had to retain information because we couldn't just look it up again in ten seconds. We built a meat-cloud inside our own skulls.

Now, the group is paralyzed. "How do you purify water? Does boiling it really work?" "Which of these mushrooms won't kill us?" "How do you actually set a splint? Like, for real?"

The Scene: The CrossFit guy from has, predictably, tried to parkour over a fence, failed, and now has a broken arm. "It's broken!" he's yelling. "I need a doctor! I need an X-Ray!" The Millennial safe space circle is trying to hold space for his pain journey.

I just roll my eyes so hard I swear I see flashes of childhood trauma. "You'll live." I walk away. An hour later, I'm back. I looted the abandoned high school library—a place no one else thought to hit. I've got the 1985 Boy Scout Handbook, a tattered First Aid manual, and two copies of Good Housekeeping from 1991.

"It's not broken, it's a greenstick fracture, you big baby," I announce, looking at a diagram. "Now shut up." I slap the magazines on either side of his arm, and, using duct tape, create a perfect, rigid splint. "There. You're immobilized. Now, try to be useful instead of impressive."

The younger gens don't know anything. They only know how to find things, and their one tool is gone. We know how to access the offline database. It's slow, it smells weird, and its user interface is called a table of contents, but it's still online.

The Analog Meet-Up (Or, How to Make a Plan That Isn't a Slack Channel)

The other thing that broke? The group chat.

The Scene: We need to split up. Two teams. One hits the pharmacy; one hits the grocery store. This, apparently, is a full-blown existential crisis for the younger gens.

"But how will we coordinate?" Chad is asking, his hands literally fluttering. "We can't use Slack! We can't share locations! What if the plan...changes?"

They are baffled by a world without real-time, constant-contact updates. Their entire planning model is based on the assumption that you can ping someone at any second. "I'm running late!" "OMW!" "Just grabbing coffee!"

We just stare. We grew up with a different, much simpler system. It was called making a plan and then fucking sticking to it.

"We're not coordinating," I say, pulling out a paper map and a Sharpie. "We're doing. Here's the plan. Team A, you go to the pharmacy. Team B, we go to the Piggly Wiggly. We are both back at this van at 16:00. Four...o'clock...PM. Not 4:01. Not around 4. Four. If you are not back at 4:15, we assume you are dead or compromised, and we are leaving. End of plan."

The silence is deafening. They are horrified. "But what if we find something good and it takes longer?" "What if we get in trouble?" "What if we just want to check in?"

"You don't check in," I say, handing them a 20-year-old Motorola walkie-talkie we found. "This has two buttons. A talk button and a not-talk button. It's for emergencies only. An emergency is 'horde at my back' or 'I found a crate of antibiotics.' It is not 'I'm feeling anxious.' We'll be on Channel 3. Don't...don't do the clicky thing."

We understood the rendezvous. We knew how to meet at the Big Boy statue at 4:00. It's a binary system: you are there, or you are not. They are used to a fluid, quantum system where no one is ever there, they are only on their way.

When you can't share your location, you have to actually have a fucking plan.

The Secret Weapon: We Know How to Be Bored

The analog advantage isn't just about hotwiring a car. That's the hardware. The real weapon, the operating system that makes it all work, is psychological. It's the one skill we mastered that the new generations find literally intolerable: we know how to be bored.

Remember a rainy Saturday in 1987? The good cartoons—*Thundercats, He-Man*—ended at 10 AM, replaced by a golf tournament. Your mom kicked you out of the kitchen. Your one friend with a Nintendo was grounded. There was no internet. There was no 500-channel universe. There was nothing to do.

So, we learned to be. We read the ingredients on the back of a shampoo bottle. We lay on the shag-carpet floor and stared at the ceiling, finding faces in the popcorn texture. We put a record on— not a song, the whole, entire album, start to finish, while reading the liner notes until we'd memorized the copyright info. We learned to live inside our own heads.

Here's the secret: the apocalypse is 99% soul-crushing, mind-numbing boredom, and 1% sheer, pants-wetting terror.

The younger generations were raised on a constant IV-drip of content. Their brains were wired by algorithms designed to eliminate boredom. A 15-second gap in stimulation is a crisis. Silence is an enemy. And in the new world, this is a lethal liability.

The Scene: Day 12. Holed up in a warehouse. It's been raining for three days. I'm sitting. Just...sitting. Watching the rain. The Zoomer is pacing. Literally walking in a 10-foot circle. "I'm so bored. This is so boring. I'm, like, literally dying of boredom." The Millennial pipes up: "Hey, guys! Guys! I have an idea! What if we all went in a circle and, like, shared our origin stories? To build community?" Bob the Boomer stands up: "We need a meeting! To discuss the morale problem!"

I don't even look up from the rain. "Shut up. All of you. You're making noise. Noise brings them. Go sit in a corner and think. Or don't. Just be quiet."

They are a liability not because they're scared, but because they're bored. They'll get antsy after 20 minutes on watch and just look around. They'll make noise just to fill the silence, ringing the dinner bell for every zombie in a two-block radius. But us? We are boredom native. We can stand watch for twelve hours, in the rain, with nothing but our own vaguely disappointing thoughts for company. And we're fine. It's just...Tuesday.

The Bridge Generation (And the Only One Left)

This is our real advantage. We are the bridge generation.

We're not analog-native, like the Boomers, who are too rigid to adapt. They're still trying to apply the rules of a world that doesn't exist anymore, baffled and outraged that the system is gone.

We're not digital-native, like the younger generations, who are hopelessly dependent on a system that just evaporated. They're paralyzed, waiting for a server to come back online that has been permanently unplugged.

We are bilingual. We grew up with one foot in the analog dirt and the other stepping into the digital stream. We're the only ones who can read both languages.

The Boomers are lamenting the world they lost. The Millennials and Zoomers are paralyzed by the loss of the tools they think they need. And us? We're just...annoyed.

When the server that ran the entire world finally, spectacularly crashed, we were the only ones who still had the offline instruction manual. And yeah, it's on paper. It's got coffee stains on it from

1993, half the pages are missing, and the cover was ripped off to use as a splint. Whatever.

It's better than a 404 error.

Of course, having the manual is one thing. Having the guts to use it—and to live with the consequences when you screw up—is another. Which brings us to the biggest generational gap of all: our relationship with failure.

Chapter 5
Failure is an Option (In Fact, It's How You Die)

The "It's a Learning Experience" Incident

The thud of the 2x4 dropping back into the steel brackets was the only sound. It was way too loud.

Outside the side gate—the one leading to the auto-shop—the scratching and wet moaning faded as the thing lost interest. I turned.

Kyle, maybe 23, earnest, still wearing pristine $200 hiking boots he'd looted, was staring at the gate. He was literally shaking.

I didn't yell. Yelling wastes energy. I just stated the fact.

"You left the gate open."

He flinched, turning to me, his eyes wide with a horrifying combination of fear and...relief? "I know," he breathed, the words tumbling out. "I know, I'm so sorry. I was just...I was checking the inventory on the truck, and I got really overwhelmed with the new system, and...I just...I won't let it happen again. I promise. This was...this was a really good learning experience for me."

I just stared.

A...*what*?

A "learning experience."

I wasn't just mad. I was calculating. This kid...Kyle...was a negative asset. He wasn't neutral. He actively drained resources (my time, my energy) and created risk. His feelings were a tactical liability. He was a walking gate-latcher, a breach waiting to happen, all because he was raised to believe that intentions were a form of armor.

He said it just like that. Like he'd accidentally formatted a spreadsheet wrong. Like his boss was going to sigh, tell him to "be more mindful of the details," and they'd "touch base on it" in his next performance review. He was actively processing his near-fatal screw-up as a positive milestone in his personal growth journey.

And that right there, that's it. That's the single most dangerous mindset left on Earth.

It's not the zombies. It's not the raiders. It's this. This earnest, suicidal belief that failure is a learning experience.

The apocalypse doesn't do learning experiences. It doesn't debrief. It doesn't circle back. The apocalypse only does dying experiences.

This is the philosophy that gets us all killed. This is the participation trophy mindset, rusted out and gone septic. The one that rewarded effort over outcome. Kyle's good try didn't matter. His overwhelmed feelings didn't matter. The only thing that mattered was the 2x4 in the bracket. He failed. And in this world, failure isn't an F on a report card. It's an E for eaten.

It was the same fucking problem as Bob from the gym, who had, just yesterday, delegated the water-purification task and assumed it was done. When we found out it wasn't, his response wasn't, "I screwed up." It was, "The system failed. My subordinates didn't execute." He was looking for accountability externally. Kyle was looking for validation internally. Both of them were failing to see the simple, brutal fact: You fucked up. You almost got us killed. There is no system. There is no learning experience. There's just the 2x4 in the bracket.

The Mosh Pit vs. The Safe Space: A Parable of Consequences

This learning experience bullshit is a symptom of a much deeper rot. It's the end-stage result of a generational divide that's been widening for decades.

The core of it is this: Our fun was dangerous. Their fun was curated.

Our entire adolescence was a case study in cause and effect. We were the last generation to grow up in a world that was still sharp, still had pointy edges, and still let kids get hurt. Our formative experiences were mosh pits and bike wrecks.

Remember Lollapalooza '92? A sea of 50,000 sweaty, dehydrated bodies in combat boots and flannel, all surging toward one stage. Remember the smell? It wasn't just sweat. It was industrial. Sweat, stale beer, pot, cigarettes, and that weird, metallic tang of potential violence. You'd get a Doc Marten to the kidney. You didn't file a

45

report. You didn't de-escalate. You just became a Doc Marten to someone else's kidney. It was physics. It was Newton's third law, with flannel.

And it had unspoken rules, rules you learned in about 30 seconds, or you got spat out the side.

Rule #1: You will get elbowed in the face. It's not a microaggression. It's a fucking mosh pit.

Rule #2: You will fall. The ground is a slippery mess of mud, sweat, and spilled beer.

Rule #3: When someone falls, you pick them up. This was the one thread of social contract in the chaos. You protected your fellow man, not by holding space for them, but by yanking them to their feet before they got trampled.

Rule #4: You are 100% responsible for your own survival. No one was monitoring the pit for safety. You were the master of your own domain, and if you couldn't handle it, you left.

If the mosh pit was our community, the bike wreck was our personal development. We all did it. No helmet, no pads, just a 10-speed Huffy and a homemade ramp built out of a piece of plywood and a single cinder block. You'd hit that ramp, get two inches of air, and the whole thing would slide out. You'd eat asphalt. The consequence was immediate and personal. The lesson wasn't "What can we learn from this?" The lesson was, "That fucking hurt. I got a mouthful of gravel, my knee is bleeding, and I have a new, profound respect for gravity." You didn't get a trophy for the effort. You got a scar. And you learned not to put the cinder block on the loose dirt. The lesson was 100% internalized accountability.

Now, compare that. Their fun was designed, from the ground up, to be frictionless. I saw one, pre-apocalypse. A 20-year-old having a full-blown breakdown because the artisanal-kombucha stand was out of his preferred flavor. Not out of kombucha. Out of the flavor. An event staffer (in a vest) was...validating his feelings. He was apologizing to him. They were trained to believe that discomfort was an emergency.

46

And now, the apocalypse has arrived. The world is now a 24/7 mosh pit, with no rules, no safe space monitors, and the zero-tolerance policy is on you.

The younger generations are standing in the middle of the pit, stunned, baffled, and outraged that it's violent. They're looking for the wellness tent. They're demanding to speak to the manager of the mosh pit. And we're just standing there, bleeding from the elbow we knew was coming, trying to explain to them that there is no system. There's just the pit.

De-Programming the Good Try Generation: A How-To

So now, we're the unwilling managers of a compound full of survivors who think trying hard is the same as succeeding. They are a liability. They are walking, talking learning experiences waiting to happen, and the tuition for that school is all of us.

It's time for a harsh, mandatory, and long-overdue de-programming. Welcome to the new (and only) corporate doctrine, the Gen X Doctrine of Results. It's simple, it's brutal, and it's non-negotiable.

First, "Good Try" Is Dead.

We're excising those two words from the goddamn vocabulary. You didn't try to bar the door. You either barred the door or you did not. You didn't try to stand watch. You either stood watch or you fell asleep.

The Scene: "Chad, you were on watch. You saw two zombies. You almost got them both. You got one. The other one wandered off...toward the farm. A 'Good Try' is what you call that...A single, undiscovered zombie in the cornfield that is going to eat the foraging team in two hours is what I call that. Go get your spear. We're not done." "Trying" is the language of effort. "Results" is the language of survival. Trying is what gets the entire night-watch shift eaten because the gate was almost latched. "Almost" is a "Good Try." Dead is the result.

Second, Your Feelings Are Not a Shield.

The learning experience is always, always followed by an apology. "I'm so sorry I wasted the last of the antibiotics! I just felt so overwhelmed!" Here's the new rule: Your sorrow is irrelevant.

The Scene: Madison drops a full, 5-gallon carboy of purified water. It shatters. It's all the water for the day. She just bursts into tears. "I'm so sorry! I just...I'm so tired and I felt..."

I cut her off. "Stop. I don't care. I literally do not care. You're crying at me. You're making me manage your feelings about your fuck-up. That's a power move. That's bullshit. Stop crying. Grab two buckets. The well is a mile away. You're not sorry until the buckets are full. Go." Your feelings don't un-spoil the food you left out. Your remorse doesn't un-fire the bullet you wasted. We are not a community that holds space for your guilt. We are a lifeboat, and you just wasted a flare.

Third, Your Capacity Is Not My Emergency.

This one is insidious. It's the language of the wellness cult, weaponized to justify slacking. It's the evolution of the feeling shield. It sounds professional. It sounds...healthy. It's the most dangerous one of all.

The Scene: The watch roster is posted. Skye (the Zoomer) comes to you, looking serious.

Skye: "Yeah, hi. I'm just looking at the roster, and I can't do the midnight-to-4-AM shift. I'm just...I'm not in a good headspace. I'm feeling really low-capacity right now, and I need to protect my energy."

Me: (A long, slow, dangerous blink.) "...Protect. Your. Energy."

Skye: "Yeah. My self-care is a priority. I'm just...I'm really at my limit and I don't have the bandwidth or the spoons for that shift. I can maybe do the 10 AM, after I've had coffee."

The New Rule: Your self-care is not a team responsibility. Bandwidth, spoons, capacity, headspace—these are all luxury terms from a world with a 100% surplus of safety. They are words you use

48

when your survival is guaranteed, and you're just negotiating your comfort.

Here? They are just a new, more sophisticated way of saying, "I'm not pulling my weight," and expecting someone else—me—to pull it for you. You don't protect your energy. You expend it to stay alive. That's the point of energy.

Your self-care is your job, to be done on your own time, so you can show up for your shift. Your self-care is cleaning your weapon and getting sleep. It's not a get-out-of-work-free card. If you can't, you're not in-tune with your needs. You're a leech with a better vocabulary. You're a liability.

My Response: "Got it. You're low capacity. So is a dead battery. Guess what we do with those? We recharge them or we toss 'em. You're on the midnight shift. Protect your energy by taking a nap this afternoon. That's your self-care. Get your headspace right. See you at midnight."

Fourth, There Are No Do-Overs.

This is the one that really breaks their brains. The learning experience mindset fundamentally relies on a next time. "I'll know better for the next supply run!" What if there isn't a next time?

The Scene: A Zoomer borrows the last can of gas...for a moped...to go scouting (i.e., go be bored somewhere else). The generator sputters and dies. The guy who's been nursing it (another Xer, of course) sprints out. "What the fuck?! The tank is dry!"

The Zoomer shrugs. "My bad. I'll...I'll get more gas next time!"

"There IS NO NEXT TIME!" the Xer screams, and this time, he's yelling. "That generator ran the electric fence...We don't get a do-over on tonight's horde!" The stakes are permanent. We have to get it right, right fucking now, every single time.

Finally, "That's Not Fair" Is Not an Argument.

"It's not fair that I have to stand watch in the rain!" "It's not fair that you get the bigger food portion just because you're on wall duty!"

The Scene: Rations are being handed out. A Zoomer complains. "It's not fair! You gave him (the guy on wall duty) three protein bars! I only got one!"

I just grab his one bar back. "You're right. It's not fair." I give the bar to the wall-duty guy. "He's on the wall. He's burning calories...Fai' is everyone gets what they need. Equal is everyone gets the same. This isn't a fucking socialist-utopia co-op in Portland. This is a lifeboat. Fair is the boat doesn't sink. Now, go pull weeds. Or starve. I don't care."

This is the new Gen X leadership style, and it looks mean to them. It feels harsh. That's because it is. We are not holding space for your failure. We are pointing at it, loudly, so you and everyone else see the lethal consequence in real-time. We are not your therapists. We are not your parents. We are just the only thing standing between you and your next learning experience. And that one has teeth.

The Audacity of Consequences

Let's be clear: this isn't cruelty. This is practicality.

We are not being mean or harsh for the sake of it. We are simply acting as the translators for the new world. We are the unwilling interpreters for a universe that, by its very nature, does not give a single, solitary fuck about your intentions, your effort, or your feelings.

The zombie horde doesn't care that you meant to lock the gate. The sub-zero temperature doesn't care that you feel overwhelmed. The consequences are all that matter.

For two decades, an entire generation was protected from the single greatest teacher in human history: failure. They were wrapped in emotional bubble-wrap, handed participation trophies just for showing up, and gently told that every failure was just a learning experience or a steppingstone.

They were lied to.

We weren't. We were the last generation to grow up in a world that was still sharp, still had pointy edges. We fell off the roof, broke our

50

arms, and learned...don't fall off the fucking roof. The lesson was simple. It was immediate. And it was permanent.

In the old world, failure meant a bad grade or getting grounded. In the new world, failure is still an option. It's just the last one you'll ever get.

So, no. You don't get a trophy for trying. You get to live. That's the trophy now.

Of course, this consequences-based mindset also means we're deeply, deeply skeptical of anyone who thinks they have a plan. Especially if they're in a uniform or, God forbid, in charge.

Chapter 6
Question Authority (Especially If It's FEMA, the CDC, or a Boomer with a Bullhorn)

The Last Press Conference

It was the last broadcast from the old world.

For some, it was a flickering image on a dying TV, the signal snowing over a pixelated FEMA official whose tie was crooked. For others, it was the final, crackling voice from a car radio, a terrified General trying to sound like he was in control. For the rest, it was the last "EMERGENCY ALERT" to ever hit their phone, a wall of text from the CDC.

The medium didn't matter. The message was identical.

"The situation is...contained," the official at the podium said, visibly sweating under the studio lights. "We urge all citizens to stay in your homes. Shelter in place. I repeat, do not attempt to travel. Help is on the way. We are establishing safe zones at your local high school gymnasium."

And in that moment, the generations split for the last time.

The Boomers, huddled around the screen, let out a collective sigh of relief. "Thank God," Bob from the HOA muttered, already gathering his insurance documents. "The government has a plan. We just need to follow the rules and wait for the National Guard."

The Millennials and Gen Zers were just paralyzed. They were frantically fact-checking on dead social media. "Is this a confirmed source?" Skye asked, her voice shaking. "This feels like misinformation! Why isn't the expert I follow saying this?" They were waiting for the right authority to validate the instruction, and the right authority had just been eaten.

And then there was us.

We were in the back, by the door, and we heard "Shelter in place at your local high school gymnasium." And as one, we let out a simultaneous, collective, guttural snort. Our brains, trained by decades of bullshit, instantly translated the message.

What did "Shelter in place" really mean? It meant "Stay in your flimsy, non-defensible, suburban-wood-frame-house until the looters or the zombies find you." What did "Help is on the way" really mean? It meant "We have no fucking idea where you are, and the 19-year-old in the Humvee who's supposed to help is currently crying and lost." And "Safe Zones at your local high school gymnasium"? That's just "We're putting all the food (you) in one bowl. Please gather in one convenient, un-defendable location so you can all be eaten at once."

The second the authorities told us what to do, we knew exactly what *not* to do. Our entire lives, authority has been a synonym for incompetent, corrupt, or just plain lying. The apocalypse didn't change that; it just raised the stakes from losing your job to losing your intestines.

The Origin of the Eyeroll: A Formative Education in Bullshit

That collective, guttural snort? That wasn't a hot take. That was the sound of thirty years of high-level, post-graduate education in bullshit.

We weren't born cynical. We were made cynical. The Boomers were born into a post-war boom of black-and-white morality. The Millennials were born into a world of curated self-esteem. We were born just in time to get a non-stop, front-row seat to every major institution failing spectacularly.

Our "Schoolhouse Rock" was just a highlight reel of disasters and lies. This is our evidence locker:

- **Politics (Watergate, Iran-Contra):** We were kids, watching *Schoolhouse Rock*, and then the cartoon was interrupted by...men in suits, looking shifty. We watched our parents watch the TV, and the adults were whispering. We didn't understand the details, but we understood the vibe. Our first political memory is a president resigning in disgrace. We learned president was a synonym for liar. By the time we were teenagers, Iran-Contra was the absurd, made-for-TV drama. "I don't recall," "I was out of the loop." We learned that all politicians lie. It's just...what they do.

- **The Media & "The Experts" (The Challenger):** This was the big one. January 28, 1986. We were there. We were

55

sitting on the floor of our classrooms, watching live. We watched a teacher, a civilian, get strapped to a rocket built by the smartest people in the world. We watched the adults wave, we watched it go up, and we watched it disappear in a cloud of smoke. We learned that arrogance and schedules kill people. We learned that confidence is what you project right before you explode. That scar never healed. It was the ultimate, horrifying lesson: The adults are not in control. They make fatal, stupid mistakes, and they do it on live television.

- **Pop Culture (Milli Vanilli):** It sounds silly, but... think about it. The betrayal. The #1, Grammy-winning act in the world was a complete and total fake. The dreadlocks. The lie. We learned that the entire fucking system—MTV, the radio, the experts at the Grammys—was in on it. We learned that authenticity is a product. We learned that anything can be faked. We never, ever trusted an award or a critic again.

- **Corporate (New Coke, Tylenol):** The "Greed is Good" '80s. We learned from the taste tests and focus groups of New Coke that data is just a way to sell you something you don't want. We learned the adults in the boardroom were just... guessing. And failing. We learned from the Tylenol poisonings that the "New, Improved!" product on the shelf could, you know, literally kill you.

- **The Local Incompetence:** This was the daily grind. This was the authority we actually had to deal with. It was the high school principal on a power trip about hats in the cafeteria or skirt length while ignoring the 10-foot, asbestos-covered pipe leaking in the boiler room. It was our first boss at the Taco Time or the Video-Hut—a 30-year-old manager whose authority was based entirely on the fact that he had the keys to the safe, and who would 100% forget to log your overtime hours.

We learned, up close and personal, that "Boss" just meant "the guy who is failing upwards." We learned that authority wasn't based on competence; it was based on who got there first or who wanted it most. We learned to manage them with shrugs and eye-rolls just to

56

survive the shift. This wasn't anarchy; it was just...seeing the wires. We saw, with our own eyes, that the adults in charge were just... kids with car keys. And they were terrible drivers.

This was our education. The Boomers had "The Man" to rebel against—a single, powerful thing. The Millennials have "The System" to deconstruct—a vast, abstract web. We just had...incompetence. A non-stop parade of clowns in suits.

So, when we're in that gymnasium, Bob (former regional sales manager, 1998) grabs the bullhorn and starts shouting, "Right! We need to form a committee!" We don't see a leader. We see our high school principal on a power trip. He's all confidence, no skill. And that, right there, is the single biggest red flag our entire lives trained us to spot.

The How-To: The Gen X Authority Litmus Test

This isn't about anarchy. We're not teenagers spray-painting a circle-A on a bridge. That's also performative bullshit. This is about vetting. We don't just reject all authority; we interrogate it. We're not anarchists; we're just...selective. We only trust competence.

So, while the Boomers are falling in line, we're running every self-proclaimed leader through the Gen X Authority Litmus Test. It has four simple, non-negotiable questions:

1. Who Put You in Charge?

- This is the big one. Did they elect themselves? The second the PA died in the gym; Bob already had a bullhorn from his neighborhood watch car. He didn't ask. He just started talking. Self-appointed. Red flag. We're looking for the reluctant leader. The person who sighed (the "Fine, I'll do it" sigh) and then accepted. Self-appointment is the original sin of the power-hungry.

2. What's In It For You?

- We're always looking for the angle. Always. Is it power? Resources? A sad, pathetic need to feel important? The only answer that is a 100% deal-breaker? "I just want to help."

- Bullshit. That's the biggest lie in the universe. A new guy shows up... He's too helpful. He volunteers for everything. "I just want to help!" he says. He's a joiner. He's a follower. He's weak. He'll flip the second a stronger leader shows up. "I just want to help" is what the cult leader says.

3. Do You Have a Plan or Do You Have Skills?

- We have an innate, allergic revulsion to big picture guys. Bob is always at the whiteboard..."Phase 1: Secure the Perimeter. Phase 2: Re-establish Comms." It's just...talking. Plans are abstract. Plans are what failed at Challenger.

- Skills are real. Meanwhile, the quiet woman...is in the parking lot, siphoning gas. We're following her, not him. We don't follow plan guys.

4. Are You Making Sense, or Are You Just Quoting a Rulebook?

- This is the final, practical test. The Boomer leader will inevitably try to re-establish the old rules. "We can't take that. That's looting!"

- "It's not looting if they're dead, Bob. It's resource acquisition. Are you making sense, or are you just afraid?" We don't care about procedure. We care about what works.

Let's run a case study—the litmus test in action. You're on the road, low on fuel. You meet a new group at a highway checkpoint. A guy in a clean surplus-store Army jacket steps forward. "Name's Sarge," he says, not waiting for you to ask. "We're requisitioning this fuel."

Let's run the test.

Test 1 (Who put you in charge?): Fails. He named himself "Sarge." He's telling you what's happening, not asking. Self-appointed. Red flag.

Test 2 (What's in it for you?): He wants the fuel, obviously. But his real tell will be when you push back: "I'm just trying to keep my people safe." That's the "I just want to help" line, but with a manly filter. Fails. Red flag.

Test 3 (Plan or Skills?): He's got a big map with red circles on it. He's talking about phases and checkpoints. He's a plan guy. Fails. Red flag.

Test 4 (Sense or Rulebook?): He used the word requisitioning. That's a rulebook word. That's authority language from a dead world. Fails. Red flag.

He failed all four tests in ten seconds. He is not a leader; he is a raider with a better vocabulary. We're not negotiating. We're not joining his team. We're just...getting the hell out of there.

The Boomer with the bullhorn fails all four tests in 60 seconds. We're not going to challenge him. We're not going to run against him. We're just... not joining his committee. We're already in the back, quietly packing a bug-out bag while he's calling his first town hall meeting to order. We're just...leaving. That's the Gen X vote. We vote with our feet.

The Bug-Out Bag Was Already Packed

This is the punchline. While the Boomers were waiting for instructions and the Millennials were waiting for consensus, we were just... doing. We were already in the garage, siphoning gas. We were in the pantry, taking inventory. We were packing.

The Boomer's fatal flaw was trusting the institutions they built. The Millennial's fatal flaw was trusting the consensus they crave. Our advantage was that we never trusted anything.

Our bug-out bag wasn't just a physical object (though, let's be honest, we all had one—a duffel bag with a Leatherman, a copy of *The Stand*, and two packs of Marlboros, just in case). The real bug-out bag was mental. It was the default-setting, hard-wired assumption that the system would fail, the authorities would lie, and we would be completely, totally, and utterly on our own.

This wasn't a shock. It wasn't a trauma. It was just...Tuesday, but with more biting.

And when that last broadcast ended, we didn't wait for instructions. We didn't look for a leader. We just zipped up the bag that's been sitting by the door since 1991, grabbed the car keys, and headed for the back roads. The plan is simple: Don't be where they tell you to be.

Of course, on your own doesn't have to mean alone. It just means you have to build a team that passes the litmus test. You have to create your own authority, from the ground up.

So that's our origin story. That's why we're not dead, not crazy, and not waiting for help. I've explained the why.

Now, let's get to the how.

Part II is where we stop talking about our formative years and start putting those skills to the test. First up: hotwiring a generator and siphoning gas from your neighbor's F-150.

Part II

Surviving the Undead (And the Living, Who Are Worse)

Chapter 7

How to Fix a Generator, Siphon Gas, and Other Skills You Can't Learn on TikTok

The Great Helplessness

The power is out. Not flickering out. Not "call the utility company" out. It's permanently out.

And it's cold. It wasn't just cold. It was the kind of damp, February cold that steals things. It was stealing the heat from the safe house. It was stealing the charge from our flashlights. We could see our breath. A kid in the corner was blue.

And Bob? Bob was chairing a committee on Freezer Spoilage Prevention.

The irony was thick enough to choke on. The universe had turned the entire gymnasium into a walk-in cooler, solving our refrigeration problem for us. The food wasn't going to rot; it was perfectly preserved in the ambient misery. But Bob didn't care about thermodynamics. He cared about the protocol for a power outage. He was trying to solve a problem that the weather had already fixed, while ignoring the fact that we were the ones expiring.

We're in a dark, suburban garage, the kind of place that smells like old tires and spilled fertilizer. The small group of survivors is huddled together, staring at the two most important objects on the planet: a silent, red portable generator, and a parked Ford F-150 with a full tank of gas.

This is the great wall. The unbridgeable chasm. This is the moment thought leadership comes face-to-face with a spark plug and gets its ass kicked.

The generational solutions are already in full swing.

Skye, the Gen Zer, is frantically swiping at her dead phone, her face illuminated by the other phone she's using as a flashlight. "I'm trying to find the tutorial," she hisses, her voice vibrating with panic. "The QR code on the generator just links to a 404 page. This is such bad user design. Who made this?"

Chad, the Millennial, is already trying to circle up. "Okay, team, let's just pause and process our feelings about the cold. I've found a PDF manual online, but it...it won't download. Also, I'm just...I'm not sure about the ethics of taking gas from this truck. Did we get consensus on that?"

And Bob, the Boomer, has found a piece of cardboard and a Sharpie. "Right. This is a failure of resource allocation. I'll chair a new committee. We need to conserve what we have. Let's form a subcommittee on freezer-food spoilage."

They're ideating, processing, and forming committee about a problem that requires a goddamn wrench.

I let out an audible, skull-rattling sigh. The kind that comes from the depths of a 1990s-era this-meeting-could-have-been-an-email despair.

"Move."

I push past them. I grab a six-foot piece of garden hose from the wall and an empty five-gallon gas can from the corner.

Welcome to Part II of the apocalypse—the practical exam. The thought leaders, the content creators, and the committee chairs have officially become liabilities. The new global elite isn't the person with the most followers. It's anyone who can make a small engine go vroom.

You're welcome.

The Forbidden Slurpee (How to Siphon Gas)

The first, most critical, and most problematic skill you need to relearn is that of the Forbidden Slurpee.

We all knew that kid. The one who could get gas for his dirt bike from his dad's mower, or (if he was a true legend) from his mom's station wagon. Or maybe we *were* that kid. We knew the simple, beautiful magic of gravity, a rubber hose, and a complete lack of supervision.

Before I grabbed the hose, I let Chad try. He'd read about it. "You don't have to suck it," he said, all Mythbusters. "You just...create pressure." He then proceeded to...blow into the hose? It bubbled, uselessly. "Okay, no," he said. Then he tried to feed the hose while lowering the gas can...into the truck bed...to be closer. He was failing

65

because he understood the idea but was terrified of the act. He didn't want to get his hands dirty...or his mouth.

The ethics committee is still debating. The design team is still trying to find a signal. We're already at the F-150 with our tools.

Here is the how-to, and no, it will not be on the test, because this *is* the test.

The Tools: One (1) piece of hose. Preferably clear, so you can see it coming. One (1) gas can. That's it.

The Physics: This is the part that blows their minds. You put the hose in the gas tank. You put the empty gas can on the ground. The can must be lower than the tank. Yes, lower. Gravity, people. It's not just a theory a podcast host told you about. It's the fucking law, and it's the only one left.

The Suck vs. Bulb Debate: Look, if you're a prepper, you have a nice, clean siphon bulb. Good for you. The rest of us are using the suck method. You put the hose in the tank. You put the other end in your mouth. And you give it two or three sharp, committed sucks, like you're trying to get a thick, frozen milkshake through a tiny paper straw. You will see the pink liquid start to move up the (clear) hose. The second it crests the highest point, you yank it out of your mouth and slam it into the gas can.

The Inevitable: Yes, you will get gasoline in your mouth. Stop. Don't panic. Don't process it. You will get a mouthful of 87 Octane. Don't swallow it. Spit. Spit again. Curse a little. You'll be fine. That taste? That's not a microaggression. It's not toxic masculinity. It's fuel. It's the taste of the lights coming back on. It's the taste of not freezing to death.

Now you have five gallons of power. You just leveled up. Meanwhile, the other gens are standing twenty feet back, absolutely horrified that we just put a car-pipe in our mouth, whispering about toxins and long-term health effects while they're literally shivering.

The Pull-Cord of Destiny (How to Start a Generator)

You've got the fuel. Now comes the hard part. Not physically hard, but mentally hard for a generation that thinks power comes from a white block plugged into a wall.

Our entire adolescence was a battle against the pull-cord. We were 13, trying to start the lawnmower. We were 15, trying to kick-start a minibike. We were 16, on your uncle's boat, yanking on an outboard motor with a sheer, repetitive, shoulder-dislocating fury. We know this machine. It's our nemesis. And our friend.

The younger gens are staring at it like it's an alien artifact. Skye is still looking for the on button. The real one.

Here's the How-To:

The Holy Trinity: An engine is not a magic box. It's a bam-bam machine. It needs three things: Gas. Oil. Spark. I didn't even go for the gas first. I went for the oil. I unscrewed the dipstick. Bone dry. "See this?" I held it up. "This is why it wouldn't start for Bob last week. He just pulled and pulled until he flooded it, but the real problem? The low-oil sensor... It's smarter than he is." I found a quart of 10W-30 on a shelf, and poured some in. Now we add the gas.

The Secret Knobs: You can't just swipe this to unlock it. You have to know the password.

1. Find the on switch. It's probably just a red rocker switch. Flip it.
2. Find the fuel valve. It's a little lever that turns the gas flow from off to on. It's always off. Turn it on.
3. Find the choke. This...this is the magic. This is the secret lever the other generations don't know exists. It's the analog version of a login. It's the secret handshake. They're looking for a button, and the answer is a lever.

The Pull: Now, the moment of truth. Flip that choke to full. Grab the handle. Plant your feet. And pull. Not a frantic, shoulder-ripping yank. A command. A single, sharp, smooth pull. RRAAA-vump-sputter. It'll cough. It's not on, but it spoke.

Now, move the choke to half. You've logged in. Now you're at the desktop. Pull again. A command. RRAAA-VROOOOOOOOMMMMM!

It's alive. The sound is deafening, glorious, and absolutely real. The garage light flickers on. You've just made fire. You are a god.

Then, the finesse. The carb. The generator is surging—VROOom-put-put-VROOom. Bob is shouting, "It's unstable! We need to shut it down!" Skye is backing away. I ignore them. I find the tiny, hidden screw on the side of the carburetor. The idle adjust. I take a dime from my pocket (because who has a screwdriver?). I turn it, just a hair, to the right. The engine note smooths out. It goes from a cough to a purr. A steady, rhythmic hum. That hum is the sound of civilization. And I tuned it with a dime.

Of course, the first time, you let the Zoomer, Skye, try it. She gave it a weak, hesitant pull. The cord didn't engage. The second time, she gave it a frantic, panicky yank. The engine caught, rebounded, and the plastic handle flew out of her grip and smacked her square in the knuckles. She's now sitting on the wrestling mats, traumatized and needs a safe space to talk about the generator's hostile and non-intuitive design. We're just...plugging in the coffee maker.

The Jiggle-It Method (How to Fix Anything)

Siphoning gas and starting a generator are skills. But the philosophy that lets you even try is the real superpower. The other generations are paralyzed because they're waiting for a manual. We don't need a manual. We have a method. This is the Gen X Grand Unifying Theory of Repair.

Percussive Maintenance: Hitting the side of the Nintendo to get Super Mario Bros. to stop blinking. Slapping the top of the 19-inch wood-grain TV to fix the vertical scroll. This isn't anger; it's intent. The shortwave radio was all static. Bob was reading the manual. Skye was Googling it. We just smacked it. Hard. On the side. The static cleared. "...weather... sixty miles west...". It faded, but we heard it. "See? Percussive maintenance."

The Jiggle Test: The sequel. The Walkman only works in your left pocket if you jiggle the headphone jack. You have to blow in the cartridge and wiggle it in the slot. It's the art of finding the sweet spot, the one unstable connection that's ruining everything.

The Duct Tape & WD-40 Doctrine: The two pillars of existence. The yin and yang of the physical world. The entire philosophy is this simple: If it moves and it shouldn't, Duct Tape. If it doesn't move and it should, WD-40. A squeaking, zombie-attracting gate hinge? WD-40. A leaking canteen? Duct tape. A splint for a broken arm? A gaping wound? Duct tape and a paper towel. It's the alpha and omega.

Open the Fucking Box: This is the big one. The other generations are terrified of breaking what's already broken. They see a sealed, magic object. We see screws. "You can't *open* that!" they shriek. "You'll void the warranty!" "It is broken, you idiot! The warranty is void. The whole planet's warranty is void." This is the ultimate divide. They see a broken-down car as a single, scary, non-functional object. We see it as a kit of parts. A source of wires, hoses, a battery, and a side mirror we can use to signal someone.

The Shop Class vs. Code Divide

This isn't an attitude gap. This is a skills gap. And it was drilled into us, literally.

We were the last generation to have shop class and Home Ec as standard, respectable parts of our education. Remember the smell? Sawdust, ozone from the welder, metal shavings, and fear. Remember the sound of the drill press? Remember Mr. Henderson, with 9 fingers, who just hated us? We all made that asymmetrical, wobbly-ass birdhouse. It was hideous. It was a failure as a birdhouse. But we made a thing. We drilled and sanded and banged. We interacted with the physical world. We learned that a machine can take your fucking finger off. That was the lesson. Not the birdhouse. The process. And the consequences.

And Home Ec? That wasn't just baking cookies. That was Resource Management 101. We learned how to sew a button (a skill that saves your winter coat). We learned that mixing bleach and ammonia creates mustard gas (a lesson usually learned the hard way). We learned how to budget for a meal. We learned that a 50-pound bag of flour is useless if you don't have yeast or know how to make a sourdough starter. While they were learning macroeconomics, we were learning micro-survival.

Then, sometime in the late '90s, that all changed. Shop became a vocational track, a euphemism for where the non-college-bound kids go. Home Ec was deemed sexist. Everyone was pushed onto one track: college. And college meant coding. It meant media studies. It meant communications.

They were all taught how to manipulate ideas, not objects.

They became brand strategists, content creators, and community engagement officers. They lived in the cloud. They were brilliant at deconstructing a problematic narrative, but they had never constructed a goddamn birdhouse.

And here's the payoff: They are brand strategists in a world with no brands. They are content creators in a world with no content. They are standing next to a broken water pump, completely fucking helpless, wondering why they can't find the settings menu, or trying to process how the pump's non-intuitive design is invalidating their need for water.

The New Skilled Labor

This is the great inversion.

In the old world, skilled labor was a coder, a lawyer, a creator, a thought leader. Unskilled was the plumber, the electrician, the mechanic, the janitor.

The apocalypse has taken that social pyramid, shaken it like a snow globe, and turned it upside-fucking-down. The whiplash is palpable.

The new alpha in the compound isn't the guy with the most followers or the loudest opinion. It's the woman who can patch a tire. The new influencer is the person who can actually get the generator to work. The new thought leader is the quiet, surly dude who knows how to purify water.

The other generations were busy building a personal brand on the cloud. We were the only ones who remembered how to fix the damn generator that keeps the cloud on.

And the generator just died.

Guess who's in charge now.

Of course, fixing a machine is easy. It's predictable. It doesn't talk back, and it doesn't need to process its trauma when you hit it with a wrench.

Fixing people...that's the real nightmare. Which brings us to our next problem: what to do when your group just can't stop feeling.

Chapter 8
The Five-Minute Crisis Protocol: Triage, Execute, Shrug

The "Oh My God" Incident

It's a moment of pure, sudden crisis. Not a horde. Not an alarm. A breach.

Dave, the Millennial you specifically told to lock the toolshed, didn't. He was processing something, probably. And now, a single, shuffling, moaning zombie is inside the compound's safe courtyard. It's 10 feet from the rain barrels.

In the 1.5 seconds it takes for this to register, the noise begins.

Skye just...stops. Dead. Her hands are visibly shaking. "Oh my God," she whispers, her dead phone already half-raised out of sheer muscle memory, as if to film it. "Oh my God. Oh my God. Oh my God!"

Bob is already vibrating with procedural outrage, his face turning a dangerous shade of purple as he stabs a finger at Dave. "Whose fault is this?! This is your fault! I told the committee we needed a better latch system! This is a procedural breach! I want a full after-action report on this! Who was on watch?!"

Chad explodes with process. He literally steps in front of Bob, holding his hands up in a calm down gesture. "Bob, stop! You're invalidating Skye's trauma! Skye, look at me, I am holding space for your fear!" He's already turning to the others. "Everyone, is everyone feeling okay? We need to form a check-in circle, now! Right now!"

It's a feedback loop. A symphony of panic, blame, and feelings, and it all happens in the three seconds it takes for me to find the solution.

And then, there's the signal.

We don't say a word. We're already moving. Our eyes have already scanned the courtyard, registered the threat (one), the location (courtyard), and the solution (nearest heavy object). We grab the shovel that was leaning against the wall—the one Dave was supposed to put away.

While they're shouting, we're already 10 steps closer, walking calmly towards the problem, shovel raised.

In a crisis, there are two types of people: those who make noise and those who make moves. The noise *is* the new problem. The noise is a processing session about the fire while the house is on fire. The Gen X protocol isn't about being a hero. It's about being the only one sane enough to grab the fucking fire extinguisher while everyone else is debriefing the color of the flames.

The How-To: The 3-Step Crisis Protocol

Step 1: TRIAGE (The 5-Second Assessment)

The first thing you have to understand is that the noise—the shouting, the panicking, the blame-storming—is a virus. And the first person it infects is you.

Your brain wants to join the chorus. It wants to ask a hundred useless questions. "How did it get in?" "Whose fault is it?" "Oh my God, what if there are more?" "Did Dave really leave the shed unlocked? I'm going to kill him."

You have to shut. It. Up.

This is our core competency. We are masters of filtering out the noise. Our brains were forged in the static-filled, over-stimulating chaos of early MTV, 24-hour news cycles, and shitty dot-matrix printers. We are built to find the one coherent piece of information in a sea of absolute, screaming, visual-and-auditory crap.

of absolute, screaming, visual-and-auditory crap.

This is the how-to: The second the crisis hits, you accept that 99% of the data coming at you is useless. The "How?" is a past problem. The "What if?" is a future problem. You have one problem, and it's present-tense.

You just have to ask the three Gen X Triage Questions. They take about five seconds:

1. What is the thing that bites? (The zombie).

2. Where is it now? (The courtyard).

3. What is the fastest way to make it not-now? (The shovel).

That's it. Triage complete. While the other generations are still loading their reaction software, you've already identified the problem, the location, and the solution.

This is the fundamental divide. The other gens are already lost because they're triaging the wrong fucking thing.

The Boomer (Bob) is triaging the blame. His brain isn't asking "How do we stop this?" It's asking "How do I win this?" He's already in a lawsuit in his head. He's building his 'case' for the 'after-action report.' He's sacrificing the present to win the past. A lethal, narcissistic-but-predictable failure.

The Millennial (Chad) is triaging everyone's feelings. "Is everyone okay?" and "We need to talk about this!" He's a trauma-EMT. He sees an emotional injury (Skye's panic) and runs to treat it, completely ignoring the physical, zombie-shaped bullet that caused the injury. He's trying to put a Band-Aid on the scream while the axe-murderer is still in the room.

The Zoomer (Skye) is triaging her personal trauma. "Oh my God!" and "I'm literally shaking!" She's not panicked; she's documenting. Her brain has blue screened. She's not a survivor; she's an audience for her own trauma. She's literally shaking because literally shaking is what you're supposed to do. It's a performance of panic, and it's fucking useless.

They aren't solving the problem. They are all, in real-time, trying to solve their reaction to the problem. We're just...walking towards the problem. We're the only ones who triaged the zombie.

Step 2: EXECUTE (The Good Enough Solution, Now)

Triage is done. You have your target (zombie) and your tool (shovel). Now comes the part the other generations are terrible at: Execution.

We are not perfectionists. We are finishers. We grew up in a world of duct tape and a prayer. We know that perfect is a fantasy and good enough is a goddamn miracle. We don't need the best plan. We just need a plan. Now.

The how-to: Stop looking for the perfect weapon. Stop optimizing the scenario. Perfection is the enemy of not-being-eaten. You don't need a flawless, 300-yard headshot. You need a $20 shovel from Home Depot...applied with intent.

Here's the scenario: A crash from the kitchen. We knew undead Bob from accounting was in there, but we thought the door was secure. It wasn't. Now he's...trying to eat the spice rack.

Chad: "We have to do something! We have to save...well, not save him, but...we need a plan!"

Skye: "What's the plan?! We need a plan!"

Narrator: (Ignoring them, walks to the kitchen door. Undead Bob slams against it from the inside. GURGLE). "Nope."

(Narrator grabs the deadbolt and throws it. Grabs a chair and jams it under the knob).

Chad: "What are you doing?! You can't just leave him! That's...that's inhumane!"

Narrator: "Bob's gone. That's not Bob. That's a kitchen-containment problem. And I just solved it. 'Inhumane' is letting that (points at door) get out and eat you. We're not using the kitchen. We're ordering out. Problem solved."

Is it a perfect solution? No. But is it a solution now? Yes. This is what paralyzes the other gens: the what-ifs. "What if the shovel breaks?" "What if the door lock doesn't hold?" We're not paralyzed by what-ifs, because we know the shovel will break. We'll deal with that when it happens. Triage. Execute. Then iterate.

Step 3: SHRUG (The Emotional Off Switch)

Triage is done. Execution is complete. The courtyard zombie is re-dead, the shovel is (messily) cleaned, and the kitchen door is locked. Now comes the final, most important step. This is the one that really pisses everyone off.

It's the Shrug.

My heart is hammering. I'm wiping...bits...off the shovel. My adrenaline is screaming. I have to manually turn it off. I take one deep, conscious breath. I force my shoulders to unlock from around my ears. I unclench my jaw. And I perform a full-body shrug—an internal and external action that says, "That happened. It's done now."

I turn to Dave, who's still pale. "You. You're on body-bag duty. Get a tarp." I don't shout. It's not punishment. It's just...consequences.

And then...I move on. I walk back to the gutter I was cleaning.

I can feel them staring at my back, horrified. Not by the zombie. By me. By the fact that I'm...not literally shaking. They think we're repressing our feelings or in shock.

We're not repressing. We are compartmentalizing. It's a high-level mental skill. We are, in real-time, taking the "That Was Fucked Up" feeling, putting it in a solid, mental-lead-lined box, and putting that box on a very, very high shelf in the back of our brain. We'll...maybe look at it later. When we're bored. Or not. Yeah, probably not.

The Lethal Danger of the Post-Crisis Huddle

You've put the bloody shovel back. You're halfway to the coffee pot. And you can feel the footsteps storming up behind you.

It's Chad. And he is furious. Not "zombie-in-the-courtyard" scared. "You-broke-a-community-guideline" furious.

"You can't just...walk away!" he's hissing, his face red. "We need to debrief! That was traumatizing! That...that unilateral action...was a complete violation of our Community Safety and Wellness charter! You didn't consult! You didn't check in! You didn't get consensus! We all feel unsafe now, not because of the zombie, but because of your toxic, go-it-alone energy!"

You stop. You turn, slowly. You take a sip of (now cold) coffee. You give him the blank, dead-eyed stare of a person who's just had to reboot a '90s-era Windows PC for the eighth time. And you deliver the single most devastating, confusing, and enraging response in the Gen X arsenal:

"...Why?"

This, right here, is the most dangerous part of any crisis. It's not the crisis itself; that's over in five minutes. It's the processing session afterward. It's the huddle. And the huddle is lethal for three reasons:

1. **It Wastes Time & Energy.** You are now being asked to stop everything—stop cleaning your weapon, stop eating—to spend two hours and a metric ton of emotional currency to process a five-minute event. That is a catastrophic waste of resources. That is energy we need for sleeping. You are debriefing the last crisis while the next one is already picking the lock. It's vampiric. You are sucking safety from the group to service your feelings.

2. **It Dulls the Instinct.** This is the big one. You are training your brain to ruminate on fear. You are rewarding panic with attention. You're holding space for the hysteria, which just tells your brain, "This is a good, valid response, let's do it more!" You're giving your lizard brain a cookie for screaming. We are training our brains to discard fear the second it's no longer useful.

3. **It Creates Therapy Culture in a Triage World.** This is the emotional vampirism we talked about. You are demanding that the group manage your personal feelings. That is not community. That is you, an adult, demanding that the rest of us stop being lifeboat rowers and start being your therapist. You are not my fucking child. I am not your emotional-support animal. We are co-workers at the 'Not-Getting-Eaten' factory. That's it. Do your job.

We are not your therapists. We are not your parents. We are not your safe space. We are, very simply, the people who just stopped you from getting eaten. You're welcome. Now get out of the way, you're blocking the coffee.

It's Not Apathy, It's Efficiency

It's time to redefine the shrug. It is not an act of indifference. It is an act of closure. It's the mental equivalent of closing a file, saving the (one) useful bit of data (Dave. Leaves. Gates. Open.) and dumping the 500-megabyte temp file of "Holy Shit!"

For thirty years, we were called apathetic, detached, and emotionally stunted. We were diagnosed by a culture that mistook our efficiency for a disorder. We just...don't see the value in dwelling.

In the old world, dwelling was a performance. It made you interesting. It made you deep. It got you sympathy. It got you a podcast.

In the new world, dwelling gets you killed.

The zombie that just ate your friend doesn't care about your grief. The Five-Minute Crisis Protocol isn't about not feeling (trust us, we saw that, and it was gross). It's about not letting your feelings win.

Triage. Execute. Shrug. And get back to work.

This emotional efficiency is a superpower. It lets us do the ugly jobs no one else will. And the most important job right now? Getting more stuff. The problem is, stuff is in places full of zombies...and other people. And we really hate dealing with both.

Welcome to the art of...looting for introverts.

Chapter 9
Looting for Introverts: The Art of Scrounging Without a Squad

The Group Project from Hell

The compound is running low on...well, everything. The dented can economy is suffering a recession. We're low on antibiotics, ammo, and, most critically, coffee.

So, naturally, a Looting Committee Meeting has been called.

It's in the garage, of course. Bob, the Boomer, is at the front with his goddamn whiteboard. He's unfurled a hand-drawn map of the local strip mall, and he's actually using a laser pointer he found.

"Right!" he barks, as if we're in a 'Nam movie he saw once. "We'll go in formation. Alpha Team—that's me—clears housewares. Bravo Team handles non-perishables. We'll use walkie-talkies. We move at 0600."

Before he can name Charlie Team, Chad, the Millennial, is already raising his hand, his face a mask of profound ethical concern. "Okay, but first," he says, "can we get a consensus on the *why* of this mission? We must prioritize the needs list. For example, is it ethical to take all the baby formula if we don't have a baby? What if another group needs it? We need to be fair."

This, in turn, cues Skye, the Gen Zer, who looks up from her (dead) phone. "Umm, that whole area is, like, *super* problematic," she says, her voice barely a whisper. "I'm getting a really bad vibe from the housewares sector. I just...I don't feel seen in this plan. Can't we just...I don't know...manifest the supplies? This feels very scarcity mindset."

And us?

We're in the back, near the door, not saying a word. We're just...quietly filling a backpack. We've already got a first-aid kit, a crowbar, and three empty pillowcases.

This committee meeting has been going on, in various forms, for three days.

This isn't a supply run. It's a group project. The four most terrifying words in the English language.

The most dangerous part of a supply run isn't the zombies; it's the committee. We have been successfully avoiding group projects since 10th-grade history class. We're not about to start now. The squad is a liability. The Looting Introvert survives by not having to get consensus on which aisle to check first.

The How-To: The Scrounger's Manifesto

This is the practical, tactical core of the chapter. This is the how-to for getting the shit we need without getting dead. It's a manifesto, and it's not up for debate.

Rule 1: Go Alone (Or with One Other Person You Don't Have to Talk To).

The Boomer wants a fire team. The Millennial wants a squad. The Gen Zer wants a support system. They all want to go in a big, loud, clumsy group.

Why? Because they're scared to be alone.

We're not. And we know the simple, brutal math: More people = more noise. More people = more opinions. More people = more, "Wait, I gotta pee," or, "Hold up, I just need to process this," or, "Are we sure this is ethically sourced?"

More people, fundamentally, means a higher chance that someone will scream.

The Gen X method is simple. The perfect loot team is one. You.

The acceptable loot team is two. But only if that second person is another Gen Xer, the kind of person where the entire mission plan can be communicated with a single, upward head-nod at the garage door. You don't talk. You just move.

The How-To: Bob's Alpha Team is clearing the building. They're kicking doors, shouting "Clear!", and generally ringing the dinner bell for every zombie in a five-mile radius.

Also, check your gear. The modern tactical gear Bob loves is covered in Velcro. VELCRO. The loudest substance on earth. You open a pouch, and it sounds like you're tearing the fabric of reality apart. It's a sonic beacon.

We use zippers. We use buttons. We use duct tape. We test our gear by jumping up and down in the garage. If it jingles, it stays. If it rips, it stays. Silence is the only armor that matters.

We are not clearing a building. We are ghosting it.

We're in. We're out. We're a shadow. We're not team players, because this isn't a fucking team sport. It's a solo mission to get antibiotics. The other gens think this is risky or anti-social or not collaborative.

We just think it's efficient. We're not lone wolves. We're just...introverts. And we're not going to let your need for a squad get us eaten. We've been successfully avoiding the group project our whole lives; we're not failing the final exam now.

Rule 2: Avoid the "Honeypot" (The Big Box Stores).

Bob's Alpha Team has a destination, of course. It's the Wal-Mart Supercenter. Or the Costco. Or the Bass Pro Shop. This is the second rule of scrounging: Avoid the Honeypot.

Where does every single, panicked, non-thinking survivor go the *second* the grid goes down? The biggest, most obvious, most well-lit source of everything. The Wal-Mart. The Costco. The Gun Store.

And what does that mean, three weeks in? It means three things:

1. They are picked *clean*. Every can of beans, every bullet, every bottle of water is gone.

2. They are crawling with the undead, drawn by the initial panic and chaos.

3. Even worse, they are crawling with other squads. Jumpy, desperate, trigger-happy Alpha Teams who will shoot you for a bag of stale pretzels.

Here's what happens at the Honeypot. I saw it happen at the Whole Foods on Day 5. A Millennial loot squad was standing in front of the last crate of organic almond butter. They weren't grabbing it. They were debating it.

"Is it fair to take the whole crate?" one asked. "That feels like hoarding." "We should leave some for the next group," another said. "It's about community resilience."

While they were having their ethical debate, a pack of feral dogs— actual dogs, not metaphors—ran in and knocked the crate over. The almond butter was lost. The squad fled, empty-handed but morally superior. They starved, but at least they didn't hoard.

We don't have that problem. We take the almond butter. We take the crate. We take the shelf it was sitting on if we can burn it for heat. Ethics are for people with full bellies.

It is the single highest-risk, lowest-reward trap in the apocalypse. It's a sucker's bet. It's the Top 40 rack. We're not Top 40 people.

We're not going for the obvious score. We're hitting the niche spots. The B-sides. The weird, forgotten strip-mall locations that nobody else ever thinks about. This is the Used Imports bin of looting.

While Bob's team is fighting over an expired T-shirt at Wal-Mart, we're slipping (quietly, alone) into the back of the animal hospital. Why? Because a vet clinic has human-grade antibiotics (Amoxicillin, Doxycycline), painkillers, sutures, and scalpels. It's a goddamn surgical center, and nobody is there.

The dentist's office. What's there? Novocain. Laughing gas (if you're feeling spicy). Gauze. Tiny, terrifyingly sharp metal tools. All incredibly useful.

The plumbing supply warehouse. The Boomers are looking for food. We're looking for infrastructure. This place has copper pipes, water filters, giant pipe wrenches (a premium zombie-smasher), and the parts to build a real water purification system.

And the crown jewel: the Dollar Store. The Family Dollar. The 99 Cent store. They're filled with the actual currency of the apocalypse: bleach (for water), lighters, batteries, zip-ties, duct tape, and a metric ton of canned crap no one wanted before the world ended, but is pure gold now.

This is the difference. It's like finding vinyl. Everyone else is at the FYE (RIP), fighting over the one copy of the Top 40 album. We're at the weird, dusty, cat-smelling record shop downtown, flipping through the Used Imports bin.

That's where the real stuff is. The stuff nobody else knows about. The stuff that's better. They can have the Top 40. We'll be over here with the good shit.

Rule 3: In and Out in 10 Minutes (The Browse vs. The Heist).

If Rule 1 is about who you bring (no one), and Rule 2 is about where you go (the dentist's office), Rule 3 is about time.

We are not shopping. We are robbing.

The difference is crucial. When the Boomer's Alpha Team gets inside a store, Bob wants to take inventory. He wants to check every shelf, compare brands, and optimize his cart. The Millennial wants to ethically source every item, spending twenty minutes debating the merits of one brand of rice over another. They are all browsing. They are all taking their time. They are all making noise.

The longer you're in a building, the higher the risk. Every minute you spend inside, every door you open, every can you drop, is a signal. You are ringing the dinner bell for every zombie and every other desperate squad within a mile.

The Gen X method is simple, fast, and brutal: You fill the bag, you leave.

The How-To for Speed:

1. Prioritize the Trinity. You are not browsing for comfort items. You are prioritizing the new Holy Trinity of Survival: Meds, ammo, calories. Anything else is a luxury. If you find a case of water, great. If you find a working record player, leave it. You don't have time to wonder if you'll need a waffle iron.

2. One Pass. No Backtracking. Before you enter, you know your target aisle (Rule 2). You move down it once. You grab what fits in the bag. You do not, under any circumstances, backtrack for something you forgot. That's how you walk into a group of people who just arrived.

3. Maximum Occupancy. You have one backpack. It should be full, heavy, and utilitarian. You are not filling five carts. You are filling one *bag*. You get in, you get the Trinity, and you get out.

The other generations are paralyzed by the need for the optimal haul. We're paralyzed by the sound of our own footsteps. We see the risk/reward ratio of time. That extra five minutes you spend trying to find your brand of peanut butter is the five minutes a dozen of the undead have to gather at the back loading dock.

"Perfection is the enemy of not-being-eaten." Execute. Get the haul. Get out. The heist is over in ten minutes.

Rule 4: Always Know Where the Back Door Is (The Quiet Corner Skill).

The final rule of the Scrounger's Manifesto is the most deeply rooted in the Gen X psyche.

We hate being trapped. It is a primal fear. Whether you're trapped by a boring conversation, trapped in a pointless meeting, or trapped by a horde of zombies, the feeling of claustrophobia and profound waste of time is identical.

We have been practicing this skill since our first high school house party.

You walk in. The music is loud. The floor is sticky. Your first move is not to grab a soda. Your first move is to scan the entire space, instinctively. Where are the parents? Where is the main staircase? And, crucially, where is the exit that nobody else is looking at? The back gate. The sliding glass door to the deck. The window in the basement.

We always knew where the back door was, just in case.

In the apocalypse, this lifelong social anxiety skill is now a powerful tactical advantage.

The How-To:

1. The Escape Plan is the First Plan. Never, ever enter a building you haven't already identified two ways out of. If the front door is your way in, you must find the busted emergency exit, the weak window, or the drainpipe leading up to the roof. If you can't find two, you don't go in.

2. The Vehicle is Your Lifeboat. If you drove, you park the car facing the exit, engine off, keys in your pocket (or on the visor). If you have to run back, you can jump in, start the engine, and drive *away*—not turn around. Every second counts.

3. The Perimeter is the Enemy. The Boomers' team will huddle in the center. The Millennials will establish a base of operations. We stick to the edges. We move along the walls, near the back, keeping ourselves constantly positioned near the unseen out.

This isn't paranoia; it's common sense. It's the ultimate opt-out mechanism. The Millennial gets trapped because they're focused on the community consensus happening in the center of the room. The Boomer gets trapped because they're trying to command the room.

We get out because we never wanted to be in the damn room in the first place.

The Psychology of Stuff (The Weight vs. Worth Equation)

You've got your haul. Now for the crucial checkpoint: the Weight vs. Worth equation. This is where the practical Gen X mind clashes with decades of societal programming.

The other generations, even in a post-collapse world, are still thinking like consumers. We are thinking like scroungers.

We are practical, not sentimental. We are not hoarding. We are assessing immediate survival value.

Look at the Bad Loot List—the stuff that will slow you down and get you killed because other survivors are blinded by the old world's value system.

- **The Boomer:** A 10-piece set of (heavy) cast-iron pans. Bob sees "investment! Good quality!" We see a twenty-pound anchor that is going to make you too slow to outrun a fast zombie.
- **The Millennial:** A framed photo that reminds them of their childhood. A heavy, vintage record player. A yoga mat. Chad sees emotional stability and authenticity. We see a profound lack of calories and a complete disregard for Rule 4 (Always Know Where the Back Door Is).
- **The Gen Zer:** A vintage Polaroid camera. A specific brand of hoodie (a comfort item). A stuffed animal. Skye sees self-expression and emotional regulation. We see a flash that will attract every zombie in the county and a useless object that occupies space needed for antibiotics.

They are paralyzed by sentimental value. They are grabbing objects that validate their *past* lives.

We are masters of the Weight vs. Worth equation. We are doing this math instinctively: Is this can of beans worth the one pound I have to carry it for two miles?

This brings us to the Gen X A-List Loot: the high-value, low-weight, multi-purpose items that prove survival is a logic puzzle, not a feeling.

- **Whiskey:** Anesthetic, disinfectant, morale-booster, and the single best barter item in the new world. It's liquid currency.
- **Socks:** This is not a joke. Socks are the absolute #1 most important-yet-forgotten item. They prevent blisters, which prevent infection, which prevents death. A fresh pair of socks is worth more than gold.
- **Lighters / Water Filters / Coffee:** The new holy trinity of civilization. One creates fire, one creates water, and one creates the will to live.

We are not preppers hoarding fifty-pound bags of rice—that's static and immobile. We're scroungers. We travel light, we find what we need, when we need it, and we leave the investments and the comfort items for the poor, slow bastards who are still trying to win the old world's game.

The Quiet Score

And that's the difference.

While Bob's Alpha Team is currently pinned down in the Wal-Mart parking lot—having a small-scale, pathetic war with another equally desperate squad over the last pallet of bottled water—we're already back at the compound. We were gone forty-five minutes. We have two gallons of vet-grade antibiotics, three boxes of lighters, and enough coffee to wake the dead.

No one even knew we left.

This isn't new behavior. We've been doing this our whole lives. Finding the one good T-shirt at the thrift store in a pile of garbage. Finding the one quiet table at the bar instead of being crammed into the loud center. Getting the one set of tickets to the sold-out show by not calling the main Ticketmaster line—we called the obscure B-side venue number that no one remembered.

This isn't looting. This is just scrounging.

And we've been the quiet, undisputed, world champions of scrounging for thirty years. The only difference now is that we're scrounging for penicillin instead of obscure vinyl.

The problem, of course, is that our little solo missions are too successful. And the other survivors are starting to notice. Which leads to the absolute worst part of the apocalypse: having to talk to them.

Specifically, the ones who need to process the fact that we're eating beans they didn't ethically source.

God. Give me the zombies. They're easier to deal with.

Chapter 10

I Need to Feel Safe: Managing the Millennial Survivor

The Canned Bean Incident

You dumped the backpack on the folding table. It was a good haul. Three dozen cans of beans (the cheap ones), antibiotics from the vet clinic, and a premium score: a full bottle of Jack Daniel's. Three hours gone, zero drama, zero meetings.

You were tired. You needed two things: a shower and silence. You reached for the Jack, ready to celebrate this small, quiet victory.

And then, the footsteps.

Before you could even turn the cap, Chad, the self-appointed Community Morale Officer, materialized at the table. He wasn't yelling. He was using his HR voice. That tone of gentle, concerned, performative authority that makes your teeth ache.

"Hey. Can we...can we talk?" he asked, already sliding a clipboard onto the table. "A few of us are...concerned. We need to have a check-in."

The check-in quickly turned into the accusation.

"Look, we're all glad you got the beans. For sure," Chad began, deploying the obligatory corporate compliment. "But we had a process. We were supposed to get consensus on the looting runs. When you just go like that, it...it doesn't make the rest of us feel safe."

He leaned in, his voice dropping to a conspiratorial whisper. "It feels...lone wolf. It's not collaborative. And...did you take all the beans? Was that ethical? What if another group needed those?"

You stood there, the weight of the last three hours of physical labor instantly replaced by the crushing existential dread of this conversation. A long, slow blink.

You had just been called to the principal's office by someone who's never had a principal. You were being scolded for...succeeding.

Welcome to the new HR. The apocalypse has two fronts: the zombies (easy mode) and the Millennials (nightmare mode). One wants to eat your flesh; the other wants to eat your time. They are obsessed with feelings in a world that is now 100% facts. Our safety is a full belly and a locked door. Their safety is a two-hour meeting about their feelings.

The Consensus Trap: Why Working Together Is a Death Wish

The core of the Millennial-run world was the process. Not the outcome, but the process of inclusion, collaboration, and consensus. It was more important to feel collaborative than to be competent.

In the old world, this was...fine. Annoying, sure. It's how you ended up with a $20 million brand activation for an artisanal seltzer, where fifty people had a meeting to discuss the font color. It was a world of ideas, not objects. There was always a bigger bank account and a longer timeline to absorb the failures of consensus.

That world is gone.

The apocalypse is a world of outcomes. There is no process. There is only: "Did you lock the gate: Yes/No?" "Is the zombie dead: Yes/No?"

The Millennial consensus model becomes a death spiral the minute the stakes are raised above font color.

Let's run a scenario:

- **Problem:** We need to move the compound to a more defensible house immediately.

- **Gen X Triage:** "That brick one on the hill. It has a single entrance and no windows on the ground floor. It's defensible."

- **Millennial Response:** "Hold on. We need to vote. Everyone needs to feel heard. Let's make a pros/cons list for all the houses. We need to validate everyone's choice, even the ones who chose the shed."

What is the result? The group democratically chooses the A-frame house with the all-glass windows because it has good light, a community vibe, and it's close to the river, which Chad argues is equitable access to water.

93

The Outcome: Everyone dies. Because a vote does not make a glass house defensible. A consensus does not stop a bullet or a bite.

Consensus is a luxury. It is for picking a pizza topping, not for triage. We are not a team. We are not a family. We are not a start-up. We are a lifeboat with a rapidly shrinking capacity.

And the person who knows how to row is in charge. End of discussion. Your need for a team cannot supersede my need to live.

The How-To: The Gen X-to-Millennial Translation Guide

You cannot fix them. You cannot change them. You cannot, no matter how much you want to, shrug them out of existence. But you can manage them.

This requires you to become a linguistic expert. You must learn their language—the specialized lexicon of HR, therapy, and feelings—if only so you can use the shortest possible words to get them to move.

Below is the Gen X-to-Millennial Translation Guide. Study it. It's the new survival manual.

When They Say: "I just don't feel safe."

- **What They Mean:** "I am having an anxiety spike, and I need the entire group to stop what they're doing and focus on my emotional state right now."

- **The Gen X Translation:** "You're right. It's not safe. That's the point. Now grab a shovel and stand watch."

- **The Tactic:** You redirect their feeling to a fact and an action. You validate the fact of danger (which they are correct about) but reject the demand for emotional labor. You give them a job that requires focus and physical action, which is the only real antidote to panic.

When They Say: "We need to process what just happened."

- **What They Mean:** "We are going to sit in a circle for an hour and talk about the trauma of that zombie breach, using a lot of therapy words and consuming vast amounts of time and energy."

- **The Gen X Translation:** "Good idea. Process this: you're on cleanup. I'm on ammo count. That's the process."

- **The Tactic:** You re-define the word process from feelings to work. You assign a tangible, immediate task that serves as the debrief. The trauma is handled by removing the evidence and securing the future, not by talking about it.

When They Say: "We need to get consensus before we act."

- **What They Mean:** "We are about to have a two-hour meeting where the least competent person's feelings are given the same weight as the most competent person's expertise likely resulting in disaster."

- **The Gen X Translation:** "Nope. This is a competence-ocracy. Susan knows medicine. She's in charge of the meds. I know how to fix the generator. I'm in charge of the generator. We don't need consensus. We need results. You're in charge of...counting the beans. Go."

- **The Tactic:** You establish that power is based on skill, not popular vote. You give them a task that uses their (limited) competence while firmly cutting them out of any critical, life-or-death decisions.

When They Say: "I need you to hold space for me."

- **What They Mean:** "I am going to emotionally unload on you for twenty minutes, and you are not allowed to fi' my problem. You just have to be present and listen to me drain your mental resources."

- **The Gen X Translation:** (A blank, confused stare.) "..."Hold... what? I'm holding a shotgun. I'm holding the perimeter. I can't hold...your...space. It's not a thing."

- **The Tactic:** This is the ultimate Gen X boundary. You treat the phrase as literal nonsense. You don't acknowledge the concept's validity. We don't hold space. We give space...by quietly leaving the room, thereby forcing them to manage their own feelings or find someone else to emotionally vampire.

When They Say: "I'm worried about the ethics of what we're doing."

- **What They Mean:** "I am feeling guilty, and I want the group to absolve me or establish a moral framework that makes me feel better about the fact that we just took some dead guy's stuff."

- **The Gen X Translation:** "Here's the new ethics: 1. We don't get eaten. 2. We don't let each other get eaten. 3. We don't cause others to get eaten (if possible). We just took that dead guy's beans? Fine. He's dead. We're not. I'm okay with that. The ethics are survival."

- **The Tactic:** You replace their abstract, guilt-driven morality with a simple, utilitarian Triage Ethics. You make it clear that the highest moral calling now is competence and self-preservation. The universe is amoral; our actions must be practical.

The Benevolent Dictatorship of the Competent

This is the final, pathetic version of the existence we were forced to live for three decades. We were the Sandwich Generation, trapped between the two demanding groups. We were caught between the Boomer bosses (who demanded respect, unquestioning compliance, and impossible results) and the Millennial/Z staff (who demanded validation, emotional safety, and constant reassurance).

The apocalypse is just the final, shittiest iteration of this middle-management nightmare.

And now, we are, once again, the unwilling grown-ups in the room.

We have been promoted to the Benevolent Dictator of the Competent. We are not in charge because we want to be (God, no). We are in charge because we are the only ones who know how to siphon gas, clean a wound, run a perimeter check, and not have a complete emotional breakdown before lunch. We don't rule by divine right; we rule by skill and emotional frugality.

This whole endeavor—managing the Millennial survivor—is the real end-of-level boss of the apocalypse. It requires more patience than a dial-up modem, more non-verbal communication than a mime, and more bites of the tongue than you can count. It is exhausting. It is annoying. It is the purest form of emotional labor.

But just when you think you've finally, finally gotten them to stop using the word "process" and have forced them to accept the new triage ethic...you hear a new, even more terrifying sound.

You're standing by the gate, looking at the Zombie-Free Zone sign you just put up. And a survivor—a Gen Zer you haven't seen since the first committee meeting—stares at the sign and says, "Umm... that sign is really problematic and you're invalidating the lived experience of the undead."

Oh...God. No.

We have to talk about Gen Z.

Chapter 11
This Horde Is Problematic: A Guide to Gen Z and Their Trigger Warnings

The Z-Slur Incident

Just when you think you've figured out the rules of the new world—survival, not feelings—the ground shifts again. You've managed the Boomer's need for a committee, you've redirected the Millennial's need for a consensus, and now, it's time for the final form of existential annoyance.

You're on the wall, training a new recruit—a Gen Zer we'll call Skylar—on basic watch duty. It's the simplest lesson in the entire course.

"Rule #1 is the only rule that matters," you explain, pointing to a lone, shambling figure by the highway. "You see one of those," you emphasize, "you shoot it in the head. We don't wait and see. We don't get a consensus. You see a zombie, you shoot the zombie."

Skylar visibly flinches. Not from the zombie—from the word.

"Umm...Wow. Okay," she says, looking profoundly uncomfortable. "Can we just...not use that word?"

You pause. The kind of long, slow, painful silence that used to be filled by the sound of a dial-up modem failing to connect.

"...'Shoot'?"

"No," she says, shaking her head. "The Z-slur. It's...really problematic. It's dehumanizing."

You feel the air leak out of your body. You manage to push three, hollow words past your teeth: "...De. Humanizing?"

You point again. The figure is now closer, arms outstretched, jaw slack. "Skylar, they are dead. They are trying to eat you."

She crosses her arms, firm in her moral clarity. "They're mortally challenged. Or the alternatively animated. And you're invalidating their lived experience. It's a microaggression."

This is it. This is the new front line. We've survived the collapse of society, the hordes of the undead, and the Millennial processing circle. Now we have to survive the semantic apocalypse.

Gen Z, the generation raised to believe that language creates reality, has run head-first into a reality that does not give a single, solitary fuck about their language.

The Great Un-Safening of the American Mind

To understand why Z-slur is more dangerous than an actual zombie, you have to understand the why. You have to understand the environment that produced Skylar.

Gen Z was the first generation in human history to be raised with the absolute, unquestioned expectation that they had a right to feel safe. Not just physically safe—that was taken for granted by the state—but emotionally safe.

This created their world, the old world (their world), which was a technological and psychological bubble.

They lived in a curated world of safe spaces, constant trigger warnings, and the glorious technological power of the block/mute button. If reality was unpleasant, they could simply demand the algorithm remove it.

This gave them profound power. If a piece of reality was problematic, they could cancel it. They could use their lexicon of semantic warfare—dehumanizing, microaggression, invalidating— as a weapon to control their environment and force it to conform to their internal needs. They learned that language creates reality.

And then, the new world (our world) arrived.

The apocalypse didn't just break the power grid; it popped the bubble. The entire world is now a trigger warning. Reality is not curateable.

The lack of power is the central, horrifying lesson they can't process. The zombies will not respect your boundaries. The horde will not read the room. You cannot cancel a 10,000-deep mass of hungry corpses by calling them a slur.

This creates the fundamental conflict.

We were taught the world was inherently safe. They were taught they had a right to safety.

We were told "sticks and stones..." and "to suck it up." They were told "center your feelings" and "take space."

We were forced to build calluses. They were encouraged to build bubbles.

We are resilience native. They are safety native.

We are about to have a serious OS conflict. They are waiting for the Moderator. They are waiting for the Admin to ban the user Zombie_Horde_44 for violating the terms of service.

They don't understand that the Terms of Service have been deleted, and the only Admin left is Physics. Their software, which is designed to control people using language, is completely useless against a world that operates on physics and biology. They are still fighting the culture war. We are fighting the survival war. And they don't know the difference.

The How-To: The Apocalypse Is Not Equitable (A Gen Z Management Guide)

This is the hardest conversation you will have in the new world, because it involves tearing down a person's core moral framework. This is not about being mean. This is about re-calibrating them to reality, as fast as possible, before their worldview gets everyone killed. This is the real, unvarnished tough love your Boomer parents failed to deliver.

We are forced to replace their moral vocabulary with the language of survival.

Concept 1: Equity & Inclusivity vs. Triage & Survival

The new world demands the Gen Z survivor replace their desire for equity (fair distribution of outcome) with the need for triage (prioritizing the living).

The Z-Survivor's Argument: The complaint comes from a place of high moral righteousness, applied incorrectly. "Your new watch duty roster isn't inclusive of people who have anxiety or time-blindness. And your triage plan is problematic. You're prioritizing able-bodied fighters over the wounded. That's ableism."

The Gen X Response (The Hard Truth): "You're right. It is ableism. Congratulations. You've discovered triage. This is not a community center. It's a lifeboat. We are not saving everyone. We are saving the boat' The boat needs people who can row. Therefore, we save the rowers first. It's not equitable. It's mathematical."

This is the non-negotiable principle of the new world: Competence creates privilege. Your feelings do not get you a pass from the job.

The New Rule: The Inclusion of Hard Labor

We are inclusive in one way: Everyone is included in the hard labor. We are not a system that distributes comfort; we are a system that distributes responsibility.

The old world promised that if you had a problem (anxiety, a fear of heights, time-blindness), the system would adjust itself around you. The new world promises that if you have a problem, you must find a way to make up for it with two units of work.

Equity means you have an equal opportunity to get eaten if you don't do your job.

Your feelings don't get you a pass. Your work does.

You need to tell them: "Your moral framework is based on a world of abundance. This world is based on scarcity. The highest moral good now is functionality. If you can't stand watch on the roof, you are now on latrine duty. It's not a negotiation. It's a trade."

Concept 2: My Truth & Lived Experience vs. The Truth & Objective Reality

The core problem is the Gen Z belief in subjective reality. They were taught that their internal emotional state holds the same weight as external, observable reality. This is fatal in the new world.

The Z-Survivor's Argument: "My truth is that I don't think the 'alternatively animated' mean to be violent. I think they're just...misunderstood. That's my lived experience of this crisis."

The Gen X Response (The Cold Calculus): "That's great. Your truth is an opinion. And it's a fucking stupid one. Here is the truth—the capital-T truth that we all now live in: that misunderstood thing

103

is trying to chew your face off. You are confusing your perception with objective reality. I don't care about your perception. I care about reality."

The conversation must be an immediate, sharp surgical cut. You must excise the internal narrative. We are not interested in the story they are telling themselves; we are interested in the physics of the situation.

The New Rule: Shared, Observable Reality

You tell them: "You can have any truth you want inside your own head. It can be your comfort. But the group operates on shared, observable, fucking reality."

Objective Reality: The zombie is dangerous. The wall must be manned. The food must be rationed.

Subjective Reality: I feel sad about the rationing. The zombie is misunderstood.

You can't eat your feelings. You can't shoot a zombie with your perception. That's the only truth that matters now. You must ruthlessly enforce the boundary between the internal and the external. The moment their lived experience threatens the physical survival of the compound, it becomes the enemy.

Concept 3: Emotional Labor vs. Actual Fucking Labor

The Millennial preoccupation with processing is annoying, but the Gen Z concept of emotional labor is the most insidious threat to the new work ethic. They are conflating the difficulty of feeling with the difficulty of doing.

The Z-Survivor's Argument: "Asking me to go outside the wire to loot is...a lot. That's a huge ask. You're putting a lot of emotional labor on me. I don't have the spoons for that."

The Gen X Response (The Joyless Laugh): You have to stop. You stop everything. You let out a slow, hollow, joyless laugh. This is the sound of existential despair mixed with profound annoyance.

"Emotional...labor? We're not asking you to mediate a fight between the Boomers and the Millennials. We're asking you to carry a bag."

Then you break down the real labor in the room:

- "You're worried about emotional labor...? I'm doing the actual labor of filling the bag and carrying the rifle."

- "I'm doing the mental labor of planning the route, watching for shadows, and making sure the gate is locked."

- "And I am doing the crushing emotional labor of not screaming at you right now."

"So...get...the spoons."

Here's the thing about your spoons. In the old world, you could trade them for sympathy. In the new world, we are literal. If you don't have the spoons to carry the water, you don't drink the water. Suddenly, it's amazing how many spoons you find in the back of the drawer.

The spoons theory—the idea that mental energy is finite and must be carefully budgeted—is a fine theory for a university campus. It is a suicide note for a compound.

The New Rule: The Will to Do It

You tell them: "There is only one kind of labor now: the kind that keeps us alive."

1. Digging a latrine.
2. Cleaning a rifle.
3. Carrying a heavy thing.
4. Standing in the rain.

The only emotion that matters is the will to do it. You must force them to understand that the pain of a tired back is temporary. The pain of a zombie bite is permanent. Your feelings are a data point, but they are not a disability. The only thing that grants you a "pass" is death.

It's a Safe Perimeter, Not a Safe Space

This is the final, most important boundary we have to set. We have to become the bad parents they never had, the ones who deliver the unvarnished, necessary truth.

You gather the small, trembling group of young survivors and give them the last piece of true education they will ever receive:

"I'm going to tell you what your parents, your teachers, and your algorithms were too afraid to say: Your feelings are not facts. You do not have a right to feel safe. You have a responsibility to create safety."

Safety is not a feeling. It's a structure. And you create that structure with work, walls, and weapons.

The Gen Z demand is for the environment to conform to their internal state. Our mandate is the opposite: your internal state must conform to the external reality. You must build calluses.

This compound, you explain, is not a safe space. It is a safe perimeter.

And that perimeter is only as strong as the people who aren't currently debating the vocabulary of the threat. We are not invalidating your lived experience. We are validating the fact that we are all in deep shit. The fact that survival is brutal. The fact that the world is, and always has been, unfair.

The good news? You'll build those calluses real fast. That's the nature of consequence. Or you'll die. Whatever.

But let's be fair. The kids didn't invent this me-first reality. They just perfected it. They had to learn it from somewhere.

Oh, that's right. They learned it from the generation that actually thinks the entire universe revolves around them. The ones who are, right now, trying to form a committee to manage the apocalypse they probably caused.

God help us, we have to talk about the Boomers.

Chapter 12

Back in My Day, We Didn't Have Zombies: Shutting Down the Boomer Power-Grab

The Mandatory Town Hall

You've done it. You successfully managed the Millennial's feelings and the Gen Z's semantics. The generator is humming, the compound is clean, and the perimeter is secure. It's...quiet. Too quiet.

And you know, with the cold certainty of a generation that has survived thirty years of suburban malaise, that the quiet is an illusion. The lack of external drama simply creates a vacuum, and something—or someone—will always rush in to fill it.

You're in your quarters, finally getting around to cleaning your shotgun (a meditative task). A shadow falls over your workbench. You look up. Tacked to the garage door is a piece of pristine white cardboard. It's written in perfect, all-caps Sharpie: **COMPOUND TOWN HALL. 6 PM SHARP. GARAGE. ATTENDANCE MANDATORY.**

Your blood pressure spikes. Mandatory? You haven't had a mandatory meeting since 2023. You thought mandatory died with quarterly reviews and team-building exercises. You know exactly who posted this. Only one generation clings to the concept of mandatory attendance at a discussion of procedural minutiae.

You go, of course. Not to participate, but to witness the train wreck.

Bob (former mid-level executive, still tucks his golf shirt into his cargo shorts) is at the front, having somehow found a whiteboard—the true weapon of the Boomer class.

Bob clears his throat. His opener is exactly the corporate garbage you expected: "Right. Thanks for coming. It's become clear to me that this compound is suffering from a serious lack of leadership. We're adrift. We're not synergizing. Back in *my* day, we had a plan. We had structure. And as the person here with the most management experience..."

And there it is. The Boomer power-grab.

The generation that *was* the manager simply cannot stand a world without an org chart. The Millennials want process. The Zs want semantics. The Boomers want control. They're not trying to survive

108

the apocalypse; they're trying to stage a leveraged buyout of it. And we're, once again, the pissed-off middle management who has to sit through their new vision.

The Manager vs. The Fixer (The Core Conflict)

This is the fundamental disconnect. This is the war of the core identity.

The Boomers are managers. We are fixers.

Their identity is built on titles, delegating, forming committees, and holding authority. Their power comes from their position in a hierarchy. When the hierarchy—i.e., all of society—collapses, their first instinct is to re-create it with them at the top. They want to manage the problem. They want to be in charge of the whiteboard.

Our identity is built on competence. Our power comes from skill. We fix the generator. We find the food. We clean the wound. We don't want to lead; we just want the thing to work so everyone will shut up and leave us alone. We want to fix the problem. We want to be in charge of the wrench.

This often leads to the inevitable flashpoint.

You'll be in the generator shed, quietly changing the oil, the only human being in the compound who knows what a spark plug gap is. Bob will inevitably wander in, hands on his hips, wearing his corporate-casual cargo shorts.

"Now, listen," Bob will instruct, despite not knowing the difference between the gas cap and the oil dipstick. "I've been thinking. You need to incentivize that engine. You need to show it who's boss. If it keeps sputtering like that, we need to have a performance review..."

I stare at him. I am holding a wrench covered in 10W-30. I am not thinking about incentives. I am thinking about the fact that if I don't tighten this bolt in the next 30 seconds, we lose oil pressure and the lights go out. I am thinking about physics. He is thinking about psychology. And you can't psych-out a piston.

The Boomer will try to manage the engine. The Boomer believes that his confidence is enough to solve the problem.

The danger of this mindset is that it's lethal. The Manager fundamentally values obedience over competence.

Bob would rather have a loyal idiot on the wall ("He's a good kid! A real team player!") than a surly, competent expert (us) who only communicates via shrugs and exasperated sighs.

The manager needs to feel respected and indispensable, which means they will shut down any challenge to their authority, even if that challenge is correct and saves lives. They are still trying to win the game that just got unplugged, and they will sacrifice the entire compound to get the corner office back.

How-To: The Boomer-Proofing Guide (Tactics for a Non-Hostile Takeover)

You've been handling this your whole life. You were managing up before it had a name, making your incompetent boss look good while you did all the actual work. This is just the final, most pathetic version of it.

The most critical rule: Do not argue. Arguing legitimizes their authority and validates their demand for a formal debate.

You use the three-pronged Gen X defense: Ignore, Obfuscate, Out-Perform.

Tactic 1: The Nod and Ignore (The De-Legitimization of the Committee)

The Boomer's number one weapon is the committee. It's the mechanism they use to seize power without lifting a finger.

Their Tactic: "We're forming a steering committee to oversee the rationing. We need volunteers. We need structure."

The Gen X Response: You do not fight them. You do not run for a spot on the committee. You just...let them. You give Bob a genuine, enthusiastic nod. You say, "Great idea, Bob. We need that oversight." And then...you don't go. You keep doing the real job.

This is the key to the non-hostile takeover: The real power isn't on the whiteboard; it's with whoever holds the keys and the padlock.

The How-To: Let Bob and Chad have their meeting. Let them ratify a charter and table a motion on the ethics of the last looting run. While they're playing Model U.N. in the garage, you're the one in the pantry with the padlock, actually rationing the food.

They are playing government. You are playing survival.

The committee quickly delegates itself into irrelevance. The moment they realize the people doing the work (us) aren't showing up for the meeting, they have a choice: either stop meeting or spend their time discussing a system that doesn't include the people who hold all the resources.

The real power isn't the title; it's the competence. We've always known this. You let them have the glory of the name, and you keep the keys to the kingdom.

Tactic 2: Corporate Judo (Weaponizing Their Buzzwords Against Them)

We speak fluent corporate bullshut. We had to. We spent three decades in meetings translating "leverage our core competencies" into "get off your ass and do your job." Now, we use their language as a weapon of deflection.

Their Tactic: Bob's face is red with conviction. "We need to circle the wagons and get everyone on the same page! We need a new mission statement to clearly define our key deliverables!"

The Gen X Response: You nod sincerely, without breaking eye contact. "You're one hundred percent right, Bob. We need synergy. We need efficiency. We need to streamline this entire operation."

Then, you turn the phrase back on him, using his own logic to get out of the room:

"We must maximize our core competencies. My key performance indicator right now is not getting eaten. Therefore, in the urgent interest of efficiency, I'm going to action item this generator repair right now. You go ahead and ideate on that mission statement. Great talk.'"

The How-To: You agree with their buzzword, then use that agreement as an immediate excuse to leave and do the actual work.

You validate the concept (efficiency, structure) while rejecting the activity (the meeting, the ideation).

Bob is rendered helpless. He can't object, because you literally just used his own corporate jargon to justify leaving the room to do something vital. He's left holding the Sharpie, convinced that he has just successfully delegated the most important task to you, when in reality, you just used his own linguistic garbage to escape.

Tactic 3: The Benevolent Put-Down (The "Okay, Boomer" Apocalypse Edition)

This is the ultimate Gen X move, refined over decades of dealing with incompetent authority: retiring them without their consent.

Their Tactic: Bob, frustrated by your efficiency, falls back on his last defense: the moral high ground. "Back in my day, we respected our elders. We didn't just do whatever we wanted. We had a structure." He's demanding the respect tax he feels is owed to him.

The Gen X Response: You give him a gentle, sincere look—the kind of patronizing affection you give a senile, much-loved golden retriever. "That's great, Bob. A fantastic story. Really. Hey, that structure sounds like a lot of work."

Then, you deliver the coup de grâce: "You've earned your rest, Bob. You just sit here and...supervise. You're the big picture guy. I'll handle the actual heavy lifting."

The How-To: You patronize them by agreeing with their wisdom. You effectively promote them to a consultant role—a position of zero authority but maximum ego validation. It's the "bless your heart" of the apocalypse.

You are honoring them into irrelevance. You are acknowledging their past status and declaring it completely non-transferable to the present reality. You have just taken the Manager and relegated him to a mascot. He is now too important to be involved in the actual work, which is exactly what you wanted.

The Manager Has No Clothes

The Boomer's fatal flaw is the deep, unshakeable belief that they are owed authority, simply by virtue of having existed longer or having held a title in the old world. They never internalized the idea that authority must be earned through competence, skill, and demonstrable results.

The apocalypse is the great equalizer. It is the ultimate market correction. It strips the Boomer of his corner office, his director title, and his corporate prestige. He is naked, clinging to a Sharpie and a whiteboard that no one respects. They are the manager who demands to speak to...us.

And who are we?

We are, and have always been, the actual manager. We are the pissed-off middle management, the reluctant technician, the one who actually had to fix the mess the boss made, calm down the staff (Millennials/Zs), and actually close up shop every night.

The Boomer power-grab is their last, desperate, pathetic attempt to re-create a world where their title mattered more than their utility.

But in the apocalypse, there are no titles. There are no org charts. There are no quarterly reviews. There's just alive and dead. And alive is a skill, not an HR-appointed position. They can manage the whiteboard all they want. We'll be...you know...living.

This is the real generational war. It's not us vs. them (the zombies). It's competence vs. chaos. The chaos of the Millennials' feelings, the Zs' semantics, and the Boomers' ego.

We're stuck in the middle, the generational clean-up crew, just trying to keep the lights on. And sometimes...the best way to do that...is to stop being middle management and start using the real Gen X superpowers—the ones we learned in the shadows.

Chapter 13

Passive-Aggression as a Management Tool: Or, How to Use the Eyeroll Effectively

The Debate That Never Happened

You are trapped.

The Location: the dusty garage. The time: 6:00 PM (Sharp—Bob insisted). The event: a resource-planning meeting you were forced to attend.

The focus of the evening is the Great Food Distribution Debate, a philosophical fistfight between the two most annoying representatives of the old world.

Bob (Boomer) is loud and rigid: "We need a top-down command structure for all food distribution! We need a single point of failure! It's efficient! It's how IBM did it in '87!"

Chad (Millennial) is earnest and annoying: "But we need a collaborative and equitable system based on consensus! We need to empower the users! We need to validate the needs of the consumer!"

It's loud. The whiteboard is involved, naturally. They're arguing about philosophy, not food. This isn't a discussion; it's a performative deadlock.

Finally, after twenty agonizing minutes of buzzwords and moral posturing, they both turn to you. You're in the corner, quietly cleaning your rifle. You are the unwilling tiebreaker.

"Well? What do you think?" Bob demands. "We have to solve this!"

You don't look up. You wait a beat. You wait until the silence is so heavy it's practically a physical object. And you deliver the single most confusing and devastating response in the Gen X arsenal:

"You're both right."

Utter confusion. Bob's jaw actually drops. "What?! We can't both be right! This is a binary!"

You finally look up, with the expression of someone who just had to explain how to program a VCR again. "Sure. Bob, you're right, we need structure. Chad, you're right, we need buy-in. Great talk."

It works because it gives them both the one thing they crave more than food: validation. Bob gets to feel like the adult in the room (structure). Chad gets to feel like the voice of the people (buy-in). They are so busy preening over their victory that they don't realize you just handed them two empty boxes and walked away.

And then, you go back to cleaning your rifle.

The argument just...dies. It deflates like a cheap air mattress. There's no oxygen, no side to take. You didn't solve the problem. You ended the conversation, which was the real problem.

Welcome to advanced Gen X management. This is our superpower. We are not non-confrontational; we are efficiently confrontational. A shotgun solves the zombie problem. A strategically deployed sigh solves the human problem. And the human problem is always more exhausting.

The Philosophy - The Emotional Economy (Why We Do This)

To understand the genius of the shrug, you have to understand the emotional economy.

We operate on a drastically different emotional budget than the other generations.

Boomers have an unlimited budget for arguments about control, respect, and being right. They will spend five hours debating who gets the last can opener just to re-establish the hierarchy.

Millennials and Gen Zs have an unlimited budget for conversations about their feelings, validation, and process. They will spend three hours processing the fear that the Boomers' debate caused.

And then there's us. We have, maybe, three fucks left to give on a good day. We are emotionally frugal. We learned to conserve energy because we were always cleaning up everyone else's mess.

We are saving our precious emotional currency for a real crisis: "The generator is on fire," "We are out of coffee," or "A horde of zombies is actively breaching the inner perimeter."

This is why an unscheduled conversation is considered emotional theft. It's Bob or Chad demanding you spend one of your precious fucks on their ego or their feelings. It's an energy drain disguised as a check-in.

What they call passive-aggressive, we call energy conservation.

The eyeroll is a shield.

The "K." is a firewall.

The non-response is a locked vault.

It's not about being immature. It's about advanced emotional budgeting. Why bother winning an argument—which costs time, blood pressure, and precious energy—when you can simply not have it?

You preserve your energy, your time, and your sanity by deploying these tools. The ultimate goal is not to prove you're right. The ultimate goal is to achieve silence. And silence is the new gold standard of survival.

The Arsenal: A How-To Guide to Non-Confrontational Confrontation

This isn't about being a dick. It's about managing dicks, efficiently. You must learn to deploy these tools with surgical precision to conserve your emotional budget.

Weapon 1: The Heavy Sigh (The Disappointment)

Description: This isn't a sigh of sadness or frustration. This is a sigh of profound, generational disappointment. It's the sound of a dial-up modem failing to connect to the internet after three tries, or the sound your car makes when you know the transmission is finally giving up. It carries the weight of 40 years of seeing this exact, pathetic scenario play out.

When to Use It: When someone suggests something unbelievably stupid that requires zero physical effort but maximum social effort (e.g., "We should hold morale-building exercises!" or "Let's vote on whether to shoot that zombie!").

What It Communicates: The communication is clear and physical: "You have just cost me 10 seconds of my life, and the sheer stupidity of your comment has given me a physical burden. I am not mad, I am weary...of you."

The Result: It makes them feel awkward for their idea. You have successfully transferred the emotional labor of the bad idea from yourself to the originator, all without saying, "Your idea is bad and you should feel bad." You just communicated that the idea is so stupid, it actually requires effort to breathe around it.

Weapon 2: The "K." (The Conversation Killer)

Description: The single-letter response, delivered via text, note, or a flat, verbal "Kay." It is the ultimate digital passive-aggressive tool, perfected during the age of instant messaging.

When to Use It: In response to a long, emotional manifesto—Chad's multi-paragraph text about his concerns, or Bob's three-page printout detailing his new plan for the perimeter. When the sender is clearly looking for engagement or validation.

What It Communicates: The communication is mathematically precise: "I have received your transmission. I have not validated it. I have not agreed to it. I have not engage' with it. This conversation is over. It is a period, not a comma."

The Result: The "K." takes all the emotional energy the sender just spent—all the urgency, all the self-pity, all the moralizing—and vaporizes it. It forces the other person to decide if their point is worth starting a new conversation, which, 99% of the time, they realize it isn't. It is a powerful firewall for your emotional budget.

Weapon 3: Strategic Silence (The Non-Response)

Description: Simply...not answering. Or, when asked a direct, dumb question that everyone else is ignoring, just staring—maybe with a slow, confused blink. This is a deliberate refusal to engage with nonsense.

When to Use It: When a group question is asked that no one wants to take responsibility for ("Who's going to clean the latrine?"). It's also effective when someone asks a leading question designed to trap you in an argument ("Don't you agree that Bob's plan is the best, or are you just trying to be difficult?").

What It Communicates: "This is not my problem." The genius of strategic silence is that it forces the other person to fill the void. The silence becomes so awkward, so heavy, that the asker is forced to break it. Nine times out of ten, they will retract their own stupid question or, better yet, answer it themselves. ("Nevermind, I'll...I'll just do it." Victory.)

The Result: You have successfully used the other person's discomfort to transfer the labor—both intellectual and physical—from yourself to the group. You conserve your energy while simultaneously getting the latrine cleaned. Win-win.

Weapon 4: The Weaponized Eye-Roll (The 'Silent Veto')

Description: The classic. It's not subtle; it's a performance. It involves a slow, deliberate tilt of the head, a heavy lid movement, and a return to the forward position, all communicating a profound lack of respect.

When to Use It: When you can't say "that's fucking stupid," but you need to communicate "that's fucking stupid" to the rest of the sane people in the room (e.g., Bob says, "We need to implement Zombie Casual Fridays to improve morale!").

What It Communicates: It's a non-verbal veto. Crucially, it signals to other sane people in the room ("Look, we all know this is idiotic, right?") and builds a silent consensus against the idea, all without a single word of insubordination. You are identifying the allies who are also conserving their emotional budget.

The Result: The person suggesting the stupidity—and more importantly, the person listening to the suggestion—knows instantly that the idea has been morally, logically, and professionally dismantled. The eyeroll is a silent, binding vote of no that costs you zero words and preserves your consultant status.

Weapon 5: Malicious Compliance (The Advanced Move)

Description: This is the nuclear option. It involves agreeing to the stupid idea with zero enthusiasm and zero common sense, and then executing it exactly as written, thereby guaranteeing failure and instantly tracing the fault line back to the originator.

When to Use It: When Bob insists his plan is better than reality, and you can't possibly argue him out of it. "Okay, Bob. We'll do it your way."

How to Use It: You follow his (terrible) instructions to the letter, without using any of the common-sense safeguards that your Gen X brain automatically employs. When it fails disastrously ("Bob, your zombie-trapping plan just trapped...us...inside the garage"), you just shrug. "I was just following orders. It was your plan."

What It Communicates: "You are now responsible for this fck-up. My hands are clean." It is the ultimate I-told-you-so without ever having to say it. You have turned their ego against them and used the consequence to secure your own position as the one person who should never be forced to follow orders.

The Sound of Silence

These five weapons—the sigh, the "K," the silence, the eyeroll, and malicious compliance—are the software of Gen X survival. The hardware is the shotgun and the generator. You need both. A running generator is useless if you've spent all your energy arguing with Bob about the proper seating chart for the mess hall.

The ultimate goal of Gen X leadership is silence. A quiet compound. A working generator. A full pantry. And no fucking meetings.

Your shotgun creates physical silence. It stops the screaming, shambling threat.

Your passive-aggression creates social silence. It stops the whining, the moralizing, the arguing, and the procedural nonsense. Both types of silence are essential for survival.

But a word of warning: This is a scalpel, not a machete.

This is advanced emotional triage. Overuse the heavy sigh, and they'll just think you have asthma. Overuse the "K," and they'll stop bringing you actual, solvable problems. These tools are for managing stupidity, not crises. When the generator actually catches fire, you don't sigh—you move.

We've covered all the group management problems: the Boomer's ego, the Millennial's feelings, and the Gen Z's semantics.

But the real art, the one we truly mastered during our latchkey childhood, isn't managing others. It's managing ourselves. It's the art of not being seen. The art of stealth. The art of...shutting the fuck up.

And that, it turns out, is the most valuable survival skill of all.

Chapter 14
Shut Up and Turn Off the Flashlight

The Safeway Live-Stream Incident

A critical supply run. It's midnight. You're in a dark, ransacked Safeway, moving like a ghost. You've got an hour's worth of training and a lifetime of instinct working for you. You are a shadow, moving silently along the "shadows" of the canned goods aisle. The only sound is the slight groan of the refrigerated section powering down and the gentle clink of your own gear (which you've meticulously taped down).

You've been at it for an hour, silent, just listening. Silence means safety.

Then, the Inciting Incident.

A sudden, blinding, bright blue-white light floods the aisle, accompanied by a booming, oblivious voice that shatters the fragile silence like a gunshot.

"Yo, yo, yo, what's up, survivor-squad! It's ya boy, Apocalypse-Chad, comin' at you live from the Safeway on Elm! Day 14! This is *insane*, y'all!".

The WTF moment hits you like a truck. You freeze. It's a Millennial from another survivor group, holding his fucking phone up, flashlight on, pointed directly at his own face...vlogging.

He's documenting his journey. He's broadcasting his exact, GPS-locatable position to the entire metropolitan area.

The consequence is instant. From the back of the store, you hear it: The tell-tale scrape. The low, wet moan. Then more moans. He's just rung the goddamn dinner bell for every zombie and every desperate, trigger-happy looter in the city block.

As Chad starts screaming—"Oh my God, y'all! This is *not* okay! This is *so* not okay!"—you're already (and silently) halfway out a busted emergency exit .

The single greatest threat in the apocalypse isn't the zombie. It's the fucking influencer. It's the generations raised to believe that if you are not seen, you do not exist.

We were raised on the opposite principle: If you are not seen, you are safe.

The Philosophy - Visibility is Liability

The old world was a contest for attention. The more visible you were, the more valuable you were. The apocalypse is a contest for anonymity. The more visible you are, the faster you die.

The difference isn't moral; it's a matter of tactical philosophy.

The Generational Divide on Being Seen:

- Boomers demand to be seen. Their identity is tied to authority and presence. They command the room. They believe their seniority is their shield.

- Millennials need to be seen. Their identity is tied to validation and experience. They share with the room. They believe their journey is worth documenting.

- Gen Z expect to be seen. Their identity is tied to morality and self-expression. They perform for the room. They believe their performance will protect them.

- Gen X prefer not to be seen. Our identity is tied to...whatever, we're just trying to get our shit done and go home. We endure the room.

Our training for this began in childhood. We were the latchkey kids. We learned this lesson instantly: Being seen by an adult (or a bully, or the principal) was always bad. It meant you were in trouble, or you were about to be given a chore, or you were about to be interrogated. We learned to move through our own homes like little ninjas to avoid detection.

The slacker trope wasn't just about apathy; it was about camouflage. We perfected the art of being the gray man in a pointless corporate meeting, blending into the background so the boss wouldn't call on us or assign us more work.

Now, we're just the gray man in a ruined city. Same skill, different cubicle. Our ability to blend, ignore, and disappear is our most

125

reliable defense. Visibility is liability. In the new world, attention doesn't get you sponsors; it gets you eaten.

The How-To - The Five Disciplines of Invisibility

You're not hiding. You're not participating in your own detection. This is the ultimate opt-out strategy for a world that screams for attention.

Discipline 1: The Shut Up (Acoustic Discipline)

The Problem: The new world is quiet. Unnaturally quiet. No traffic, no hum of AC units, no endless ringtone chorus. This means every sound you make travels. A dropped canteen sounds like a grenade.

Their Failure: The other generations narrate their lives. They think out loud. They gasp, they shriek, they might accidentally answer their dead phone. They will talk to the zombies ("Get away from me!"). They will whistle a nervous tune. They are acoustically incontinent.

The Gen X Rule: Don't. Fucking. Talk. Communication should be limited to the other great Gen X superpower: the "I-can't-believe-this-sht" non-verbal glance. A raised eyebrow is silent. A pointed finger is silent. Remember, the sigh is a social tool; in the field, it's a death sentence.

The How-To (Tactical Silent Prep): You need to secure everything on your pack. No dangling canteens or mag pouches. Wrap your keys and loose carabiners in tape. Your zipper pulls must be muffled. The sound of your boot on gravel should make *you* flinch. You are a ghost. Ghosts don't hum 'Smells Like Teen Spirit.'.

And a special note for the Boomers: You have to suppress the dad noise.

You know the one. It's the involuntary "HHHNNNGGG" grunt you make every time you stand up, sit down, or lift something heavier than a remote control. It is a biological siren song. To a zombie, that groan sounds like a dinner bell. It says, "Here is a large, slow meal that is already in pain."

126

We have bad knees too. We have bad backs. But we learned to suffer in silence. Swallow the grunt. If you stand up, you do it silently. If you can't, stay in the chair.

Discipline 2: The Turn Off the Flashlight (Light Discipline)

The Problem: The new world is dark. The old world's light pollution is gone, making the darkness profound and absolute. This means every light you introduce—no matter how small—is a beacon visible for miles.

Their Failure: They can't stop using the light. It's the phone-as-face-flashlight (the one Chad was using). It's the "I'm scared" headlamp. They have an emotional, non-negotiable need to see everything at once. They are trained to fear the darkness itself.

The Gen X Rule: Embrace the fucking dark. We grew up in it. We rode bikes home at dusk with no lights. We knew how to get a glass of water from the kitchen at 2 AM without turning on a single light. We know that the darkness is your ally and your camouflage.

The How-To: Your eyes adjust. It takes twenty minutes. Let them. Do not rush the process. If you absolutely must use light, you use it for one second to identify something (e.g., "Is that a can of beans or cat food?"), then kill it. Never use it to navigate. Never use it at all if you can help it. If you have a headlamp, use a red filter or cover it with your hand to direct a tiny beam. You are not reading in the dark; you are moving. Act like it. The reward is invisibility. The penalty for failure is a spotlight on your face.

Discipline 3: The Carpet-Shark (Movement Discipline)

The Problem: People walk like elephants. They heel-strike. They stomp. They slam doors because they expect the world to get out of their way.

Their Failure: The Boomer walks with the heavy, flat-footed confidence of ownership. Clomp, clomp, clomp. The Millennial/Zoomer shuffles, dragging their feet because they're looking at a screen (even if it's imaginary). Both are loud.

The Gen X Rule: Walk like you're sneaking in at 2 AM. We know this walk. It's the walk you used when you missed curfew by an hour and had to get from the front door to your bedroom without waking your dad. It is the carpet-shark shuffle."

The How-To:

- **The Roll:** You don't step; you roll. Outside edge of the foot first, then roll to the inside. It distributes the weight. No thuds.
- **The Test:** You don't commit your weight until you've tested the floorboard. If it creaks, you don't step there. You step three inches to the left.
- **The Doorknob:** You never, ever just turn and push a doorknob. You grab it. You apply upward pressure to lift the latch off the striker plate. You turn it slowly. You push. You release slowly. A clicking latch is a gunshot.

We navigated entire houses filled with creaky hardwood and sleeping, angry parents without making a sound. Avoiding a zombie in a warehouse is easy; avoiding a dad waking up to check the thermostat was the real training.

Discipline 4: The Sephora Ban (Olfactory Discipline)

The Problem: Zombies hunt by smell. And modern humans smell ridiculous.

Their Failure: The comfort item problem again. The Zoomer wants to apply their essential oils for anxiety. The Millennial is using artisanal beard balm with notes of sandalwood and cedar. The Boor is wearing enough Old Spice to embalm a pharaoh.

The Gen X Rule: Smell like Dirt. Or Nothing.

The How-To: Stop washing your clothes with spring meadow detergent. Stop wearing deodorant that smells like arctic rush. If you smell like a cucumber-melon salad, you are begging to be eaten. You need to smell like the world: dust, oil, stale sweat, and rain. If you can smell yourself, the zombie smelled you a mile ago.

Discipline 5: The Kill Your Vlog (Mental Discipline)

The Problem: The most insidious habit is the compulsion to document, share, and perform. This is the final frontier of distraction.

Their Failure: They are performers in their own apocalypse movie. They are constantly thinking about the story they will tell later, not the situation they are in now. This is the continuous partial attention in its most lethal form. Their consciousness is split between the rifle scope and the imagined comment section.

The Gen X Rule: You are not documenting the crisis; you are surviving it. Get your head out of the narrative and into the room. There is no audience. There is no applause. There is only life and death, and only one of those outcomes makes for a good follow-up video.

The How-To (The Final Disconnect): The only story that matters is the one where you don't die. Stop thinking about how you'll describe this later and focus on the fucking doorknob in front of you. That phone in your pocket? It's not a tool. It's a liability. It's a noisemaker, a light source, and a constant invitation to distraction. Turn it off. Put it in the bottom of your bag. You are not live streaming the end of the world. You are living it. Act accordingly.

The Curse Is the Cure

This is the final, ultimate Gen X survival skill. It's the synthesis of our entire origin story: The latchkey privilege created the emotional self-sufficiency, and the decades of being ignored created the invisibility.

For thirty years, our invisibility was our curse. We were the forgotten generation. The slackers. The apathetic middle children nobody paid attention to. We were a demographic rounding error. Our complaints were ignored. Our music was dismissed. Our aesthetic was meh.

Now, in a world where attention gets you killed, our curse has become our single greatest weapon.

They can't kill what they can't see. They can't argue with what they can't find. They can't give notes to a ghost.

This is the victory.

The Boomer wants to command the room.

The Millennial wants to process with the room.

The Z wants to be validated by the room.

The Gen X-er just wants to leave the room, unnoticed, with a bag full of canned soup. That is the ultimate goal.

And so, Part II concludes. You've survived. You've used your childhood trauma, your apathy, your analog skills, your toughness, your skepticism, your practical know-how, your crisis management, your scrounging, your HR-from-Hell, your emotional efficiency, and your invisibility.

You're alive.

...Shit. Now what?.

Now comes the hard part. We...ugh...we have to rebuild.

Part III
Rebuilding the World (Because Someone Has To, Apparently)

Whatever, Just Don't Be an Asshole

Article I: Pull Your Weight

Article II: Don't Be Loud

Article III: Don't Touch My Stuff

Article IV: We're Not Debating It

Chapter 15
The New Constitution: The Whatever, Just Don't Be an Asshole Doctrine

The Constitutional Convention That Wasn't

You made it.

The zombies are thinned out. The walls are secure. The generator—which, yes, you fixed—is running its glorious, low-grade hum. The daily rhythm is established. For the first time in a year...it's boring.

And this, of course, is when the real problems start.

You are sitting quietly, enjoying a moment of hard-won peace, when Bob (Boomer) and Chad (Millennial) approach you. They look, unbelievably, serious. Like they're about to unveil a new strategic partnership in which you are required to invest heavily.

"We need to talk," Bob begins, adjusting his cargo shorts. "It's time to codify our new society. We need a charter. A bill of rights. We need a government."

The old world relapse is immediate and nauseating. Before you can even finish your terrible, but your coffee, they've hauled out a whiteboard (where do they keep finding these things?).

"Bob and I have been talking," Chad beams, holding a multi-colored dry-erase marker. "We think we should schedule a week of town halls to ratify a new constitution. We can base it on the U.S. Constitution, but, like...better."

And here comes the final, inevitable voice of the old world. Skye (Gen Z) appears and chimes in: "And the preamble must include a land acknowledgment and a clear definition of our community's emotional-safety guidelines..."

The collective noise of procedure and self-importance hits you, and you finally finish your coffee. You set the mug down, deliberately, slowly.

The Gen X Veto is a single word. "No."

Utter confusion. Bob stammers, "What do you mean, 'no'? This is civilization! This is process! This is law!"

You look up, giving them the expression of someone who just had to explain for the third time how to properly insert a cassette tape into

134

a Walkman. "Sure. You're all trying to re-create the exact, fucking, over-complicated system that collapsed."

You're building a civilization based on meetings, subcommittees, and arguments about semantics. You're building a world designed to be debated, not lived in.

"We're not doing that," you state flatly. "The constitution is already written. It's simple. It's done. It's the Whatever, Just Don't Be an Asshole Doctrine. And it's not up for debate."

The Philosophy - The Minimal Viable Government

The old world died of complication. It died of bureaucracy, lobbying, emotional overhead, and semantic quicksand. It was a system that relentlessly incentivized the worst people—the loudest, the neediest, the most power-hungry. It was a massive machine built to turn good work into meetings, and good ideas into endless debate.

We are not repeating that mistake.

The goal of the new government isn't growth or justice or equity or greatness. The goal is peace. A quiet, functional, low-drama existence. We're not building a nation. We're building a compound that doesn't suck.

This brings us to the Whatever, Just Don't Be an Asshole (WJDBAA) Doctrine.

It's not a legal system; it's a filter. It's an operating system for adults. It assumes competence and self-reliance as the default setting. The old system had to manage children—it had to monitor every move, document every incident, and constantly enforce complex rules because it assumed failure. This new system trusts adults.

If you act like a child (by being an asshole), you've violated the doctrine. Simple. No sub-committees needed to interpret the intent.

This is the great shift: The old world was obsessed with your rights. The new world is obsessed with your responsibilities.

Your rights—the right to eat, the right to shelter, the right to not be shot—are what's left over after you've met your responsibilities. And your primary, non-negotiable responsibility, the foundation of this entire society, is...not being an asshole.

The Four (and Only Four) Articles of the New Constitution

You want a charter? Fine. Here's your fucking charter. It has four rules. That's it. It's written with the appropriate level of exasperation, and it functions perfectly.

Article I: Pull Your Weight.

This is the foundation of the new economy and the new social contract. It defines survival as a meritocracy of effort.

What It Means: Competence is the new currency. Your value is not your identity, your title, your followers, or your feelings. Your value is what you can do.

Can you fix the fence? Can you grow food? Can you stand watch? Can you teach a skill? Can you be quiet? If the answer is yes, you are a net positive. If the answer is no, you are a problem. Think of it as an exchange rate. One hour of fixing the water pump is worth infinite hours of giving feedback on the water pump. One dead zombie is worth infinite thoughts and prayers. We trade in tangible assets now.

The Crime: The crime isn't failure; it's being a leech.

This isn't just about food; it's about emotional and social leeching. The crisis creator, the committee former, the trauma processor. If your entire contribution is making other people manage you, you are not pulling your weight. You are consuming time, energy, and emotional bandwidth that could be used to, you know, survive.

The Consequence: The consequence is clear, immediate, and utterly lacking in process.

If you contribute, you eat. If you can't contribute, we'll teach you. If you won't contribute...the gate's over there. Good luck.

We are not running a social program. We are running a lifeboat. Every person must be a functional component. You either pull your weight, or the weight pulls you down.

136

Article II: Don't Be Loud.

This article is the antidote to the main character syndrome that killed the old world. It is the core rule for maintaining that hard-won silence.

What It Means: This isn't just acoustic; it's emotional and spiritual. Don't be spiritually loud.

Don't start screaming matches in the mess hall. Don't engage in political grandstanding. Don't demand everyone look at you. Don't make your internal crisis everyone's external problem. Don't be dramatic. We're all tired.

The Crime: The crime is main character syndrome. The belief that your emotions, your problems, or your opinions are so vastly important that the entire compound must pause and listen. The world does not revolve around you. You are not the star of the apocalypse. You are an extra, just like everyone else. Your needs do not supersede the entire group's need for peace and quiet.

The Consequence: This is the ultimate Gen X punishment. We're not your therapists. We're not your audience. Handle your shit. If you get loud, you will be ignored.

We will not scream back. We will not debate. We will simply turn our backs and walk away. That active, collective indifference is a far more effective consequence than any physical punishment. The person who needs the attention will receive nothing but the cold, hard shoulder of the entire group. That's the power of the WJDBAA doctrine.

Article III: Don't Touch My Stuff.

This article is the foundation of personal liberty and boundaries in the new society. It is the final defense against the collapse into petty, resource-draining communalism.

What It Means: The foundation of the new society is radical, non-negotiable autonomy and boundaries. My stuff, my space, my time. Your stuff, your space, your time.

This is not a fucking commune unless we all agreed it was. Since we didn't, my rifle is mine. My coffee stash is mine. My hour of quiet time is mine.

The Crime: The crime is forced communalism. This is the Boomer who borrows your one good hammer without asking. This is the Millennial who wants to equitably redistribute your private stash of whiskey for the good of the group (after they wasted theirs on a stupid party). This is the absolute violation of the social contract of respect.

The Consequence: This is the only rule that has an immediate, physical consequence. It is the one thing we will get loud about.

Mine is mine. Yours is yours. That's the equity we've all been talking about. It's the social contract of not being a thieving asshole.

If you violate this rule, you have demonstrated that you are a threat to the foundation of the compound. We are not a court of law. We are a lifeboat. And we do not tolerate pirates.

Article IV: We're Not Debating It.

This is the enforcement clause for the entire doctrine. This is the death of process as a hobby. This is the anti-filibuster clause.

What It Means: This rule exists to protect the other three rules. This is the line that separates a functional society from a permanent town hall meeting.

The Crime: The crime is trying to litigate the first three rules:

1. "Well, what's the legal definition of loud?"

2. "What's the appeal process for being labeled an asshole?"

3. "I'd like to form a subcommittee on Article I to establish clearer metrics..."

The moment you try to form a subcommittee to debate whether or not you're an asshole, you have demonstrated that you are, in fact, an asshole and are being spiritually loud.

The Consequence: The moment you try to form a subcommittee, you're in violation of Article II. It's a self-correcting system.

We're not having a meeting about it. The debate is the crime. We're just...shrugging and walking away from you. This is the final, non-negotiable step to securing the peace: The system works, shut up.

The Utopia of Whatever

So, there's your government. It's not a charter. It's a vibe. It's a shrug. It's a social contract that was blessedly unspoken for thirty years (until now, because you fuckers made me articulate it).

This is the ultimate Gen X achievement: the utopia of Whatever.

The benefit is immediate and profound: a world free of assholes. A world where competence is rewarded, drama is punished, boundaries are respected, and meetings are a capital offense.

This is a society built on the principle of low emotional overhead and high functionality. We are not shooting for greatness; we are shooting for sustainable, minimal annoyance.

The ultimate victory is not power; it's peace. It's a world where you are finally, blessedly, left alone.

And if you're not an asshole, it's paradise. If you *are* an asshole...well, you're free to go start your own compound. We hear Bob and Chad are already workshopping a name for theirs. Good for them. They'll be dead in a week.

With the government sorted (by not having one), we can finally get to the real work. Rebuilding a world that's not just functional, but...dare we say it...not terrible. A world where you don't have to be a hero. You just have to be...a person.

Which leads us to the next, and potentially most profound, Gen X philosophy: The Art of Mediocrity.

Chapter 16
The Art of Mediocrity: Why You Don't Need to Be a Hero

The Hero vs. The Plumber

You're trapped in the familiar purgatory of a compound meeting (you still don't know why you agreed to these). But this time, the problem isn't process; it's performance.

A survivor—let's call him Blaze—is standing on an upside-down crate, giving a full-throated, cinematic speech. He's young, annoyingly charismatic, and his hair is inexplicably perfect. He just got back from a daring (read: stupid) run.

The hero speech is pure, unadulterated nonsense: "They had us pinned down! But we fought! We bled! We are the tip of the spear! We will not live in fear! We will take back this city!" The younger, dumber survivors cheer, their eyes shining with borrowed glory.

Skye is filming it, of course, framing Blaze against the sunset. Chad is nodding, murmuring "Yes, king, speak your truth." Bob is taking notes, planning to appoint Blaze as VP of Perimeter Operations.

You just check your watch. You calculate that this speech has cost the group approximately 40 man-hours of labor that could have been used to reinforce the gate. You are doing the math of charisma, and the ROI is terrible.

You, meanwhile, are in the back, checking the inventory sheet. You know the hero cost of Blaze's last fifteen minutes of drama: two gallons of precious, siphoned gas, one kid with a freshly broken leg, and the entire haul was a box of cheap cigars and a single (expired) bag of Tostitos.

Blaze is a symbol. He's also an idiot.

While Blaze is speechifying, you notice Sarah (another X-er) quietly slip out the back. You follow her. She's behind the mess hall with a wrench. The main water pipe from the cistern is leaking—a slow, persistent drip that would have become cholera in a week.

She's methodically tightening a joint. It is boring, unglamorous, silent work. The only sounds are the scrape of the wrench and her low exhale.

The clincher arrives when the leak stops. Sarah wipes grease on her pants. "If that pipe had burst," she mutters, "we'd all be drinking ditch water in three days." She just saved everyone. There were no speeches. No one will ever know.

The thesis is simple: The apocalypse is full of heroes like Blaze. They look great. They give great speeches. They get people killed. The old world loved them. The new world is saved by people like Sarah. The mediocre. The quiet ones. The plumbers, the filter-cleaners, the menders, the watchers. The world isn't saved by the anti-zombie squad; it's saved by the anti-cholera squad.

This chapter is a love letter to the gloriously, functionally mediocre.

The Philosophy - The Rick Grimes Is a Liability

The old world was obsessed with heroes, leaders, visionaries, and personal brands. The apocalypse is lethal for them. The world of Blaze—the hero—is a profound tactical failure, destined for dramatic collapse.

Here is why the hero is a problem, not a solution:

1. **Heroes Are Loud:** A hero violates Article II of the New Constitution. They are inherently dramatic. They need the spotlight. They have feuds, they give speeches, and they are masters of the high-stakes confrontation. They are emotional vampires who demand your attention and energy to sustain their narrative. While you're focusing on filtering the water, they're demanding you focus on their inner turmoil.

2. **Heroes Are Unstable:** A Hero fundamentally needs a crisis. Their identity is built around the moment of glory, the dramatic rescue. In the absence of a crisis, they will create one. They can't tolerate boring—and boring is the entire goal of the new world. They will challenge the perfectly functional system, or go on a daring run just to feel something. They mistake stability for stagnation, and their need for personal narrative will always supersede the compound's need for peace.

3. **Heroes Are Inefficient:** Heroes don't work; they perform. They will lead the charge, but they won't clean the guns

143

afterward. They will inspire the farmers, but they won't weed the garden. They consider themselves above the mediocre work—the plumbing, the cleaning, the watch duty—that actually keeps people alive. They are net energy consumers.

The Slacker Re-Defined as the Functionalist

We, the forgotten generation, have the answer.

Our so-called apathy was never laziness. It was an allergy to bullshit. We just wanted to do the work, get the paycheck, and be left alone.

The apocalypse is the greatest "bullshit cleanse" in history. The meetings, the vision, the branding—it's all gone. All that's left is the work.

We're not slackers; we're functionalists. We're the only ones who instinctively know that a working water filter is more valuable than a rousing speech. The world isn't saved by the dramatic hero at the gate; it's saved by the person quietly fixing the hinge in the back.

The How-To - A Guide to Virtuous Mediocrity (The Anti-Influencer)

Your new ambition is not greatness. It's usefulness. Your goal is to be so competent and so reliable that you are left the fuck alone. That, my friend, is the new C-Suite.

Step 1: Embrace the Boring Job.

This is the deliberate choice to become a functional gray entity. It requires humility and a complete divorce from the need for attention.

The Argument: Find the least sexy, least brandable job in the compound. The one no one ever vlogs about. Wall maintenance. Seed sorting. Latrine digging. Water filtration. Mending clothes. This is the real power.

The Roster of Glory: While Blaze and Chad are arguing about who gets to man the observation tower (high drama, high visibility, low actual utility), you quietly take over the septic field maintenance. You volunteer to fix the damp spot in the roof. You are the person who handles the inventory of cleaning supplies.

The Why (Total Autonomy): You gain power through indispensability and lack of glamour. Nobody will ever fuck with you. Nobody wants your job. Nobody understands your job. They will never replace you. They will never manage you. You have just achieved total autonomy by becoming the sewer guy.

The Uniform of Invisibility: Don't wear the tactical gear. Don't wear the cool leather jacket. Wear coveralls. Wear something stained with grease or dirt. If you look like you are already doing a dirty job, people will instinctively avoid making eye contact with you because they are terrified you will ask for help. A clipboard and a frown are the ultimate Do Not Disturb sign.

The generator doesn't need inspiration from a charismatic leader; it needs oil from a technician. Be the oil. Be the quiet, non-negotiable component that, if removed, causes immediate, catastrophic failure. You don't get a medal, but you get to sit down when your shift is over.

Step 2: Reject the Personal Brand.

This is the anti-influencer ethos. The old world's religion was the personal brand: Who are you? What is your narrative? What are your aesthetics? In the new world, the personal brand is a liability, a target painted on your back.

The Argument: Your brand is reliability. Your brand is that person who knows how to fix the radio but doesn't make a big deal about it.

The How-To: When someone asks what you do in the compound, the correct Gen X answer is: "Stuff." Or: "A bit of everything." Or just a shrug.

You must eliminate all drama and self-aggrandizement.

Do not give your small, functional team a cool name (like Blaze's "Wolf Pack").

Do not narrate your work—you don't need a witness when you're cleaning the grease trap.

Do not take credit. The generator came on? "It just needed oil." The pipe stopped leaking? "It was just a loose joint."

The hero wants credit. They crave the applause, the validation, and the post-run emotional processing.

The mediocre (you) wants coffee and quiet. You want the functional reward—the hot beverage and the uninterrupted silence—not the social reward. You are building systems that function without your presence, which is the only way to achieve true freedom.

Step 3: Master Detached Expertise (The Apathy Advantage).

The final step in achieving virtuous mediocrity is synthesizing your competence with your apathy. You must become the ultimate utility.

The Argument: You are an expert. You're the only one who knows how to jerry-rig the solar panels to the main grid. But you must not be an asshole about it. You are not a visionary; you are a technician. You separate your skill from your ego.

The How-To: When they ask for your opinion on the failing grid, you don't give a speech about the fate of the compound. You give a diagnosis: "The inverter's fried. It'll take two hours and the soldering iron from my bag."

You are not caring about the fate of the world. You are caring about the soldering joint.

This detached mindset is how you avoid burnout, stay sane, and actually fix the goddamn problem. The Hero (Blaze) internalizes the crisis—"The fate of the compound rests on my shoulders!"—and paralyzes himself. The Technician (you) externalizes the problem— "The inverter is a broken thing I can fix"—and remains functional.

Your emotional indifference is a self-preservation tool. It ensures that when everyone else is running on empty from emotional exhaustion, you still have the clear focus required to keep the lights on.

The Janitor Is the New King

Let's summarize the great reversal.

In the old world, we were the middle managers and functional cogs propping up the visionary Boomer CEOs and influencer Millennials. We were the mediocre ones who actually made the spreadsheets work. In the new world, all the pretend jobs are gone. Brand strategist, thought Leader, synergy consultant—they're all zombie food.

The great reversal is complete. All that's left are the real jobs. The functional jobs. The mediocre jobs.

The janitor is more important than the Senator.

The plumber is more valuable than the influencer.

The filter-cleaner (Sarah) is the new king.

The hero will eventually get himself (and his wolf pack) eaten. It's inevitable. And that night, after the sad speeches and the moment of silence, someone will still have to clean the water filter.

That someone will be you. You're not the hero. You're the survivor. You're the reason there's a tomorrow. You are gloriously, functionally, and successfully mediocre.

So, how do we build a society that lasts? We don't build it on heroes. We build it on this: competence. We build it on work.

Which means we have to...ugh...teach. We have to start re-educating the survivors who were taught that feelings trump fixing.

148

Chapter 17

Re-Education, Gen X Style: Home Ec, Shop Class, and How to Be Bored

The Ideation Incident

With the WJDBAA Doctrine in place, the fighting stopped. The systems worked. But now came the maintenance of the system.

You're trying to build a new garden bed—the crucial, next step for long-term food stability. You've got lumber, a saw, a hammer, and nails. You asked two of the younger survivors—Aiden (Millennial) and Skye (Gen Z)—to help. It's simple labor. You measure twice, cut once, and nail.

You turn around to grab a level. When you turn back, you find them standing in a circle, talking. They have a stick and are drawing diagrams in the dirt.

The WTF dialogue begins.

"What are you doing? I need this frame built now," you state, holding up the two-by-four.

Aiden sighs with patience. "We're just in a sprint to ideate the most frictionless solution for the frame's integrity. Skye is concerned that the user story of the plant isn't being centered in this build."

Skye nods solemnly. "And like, the aesthetic is very problematic. It's just...boxes. I don't feel passion-aligned with this project. It feels...structurally traditional."

You feel the hollow despair sink in. You take the hammer from the ground. You pick up a nail. You slam it into the wood with a deafening WHAM.

"This," you state, driving the second nail in with another WHAM, "is passion. This," another WHAM, "is ideation. This," you point to the joined corner, "is centering the user story. You've been educated into total fucking uselessness."

The thesis is clear: The old world's education system wasn't just broken; it was a suicide pact. It taught them how to deconstruct but not how to build. It taught them how to feel but not how to fix. They were critical thinkers who would starve to death looking at a can with no opener.

It was time for a new core curriculum. It was time for re-education, Gen X style.

The Philosophy - The Anti-Curriculum

The old system was obsessed with college and thought leadership, which was just a massive, abstract pipeline for creating bullshit jobs. It was a system built on abstraction and validation—it rewarded knowing how to talk about fixing the problem, not how to fix the problem.

We are implementing the anti-curriculum.

The Gen X goal is clear and 100% vocational. It's not about finding your passion. It's about being useful. It's not about getting an A. It's about not dying. The goal is not to create scholars or critics. It is to create functional, non-annoying adults.

Our teaching credentials are the most legitimate in the new world. We are the masters of the last era of consequences. Our degree is our entire childhood. We were educated by benign neglect, broken appliances, and sheer, profound boredom. We are graduates of the School of Hard Knocks—or, more accurately, the School of 'Ugh, Fine, I'll Do It Myself.'"

The campus is the compound. The final exam is every day. The tuition is you get to eat.

There is no tenure, and there are no fucking safe spaces. We are replacing the need for validation with the simple, satisfying reality of a job well done. The bell doesn't dismiss you; the completed task does.

The New Core Curriculum (The Three Departments)

Welcome to Gen X University. Your major is Not Dying. Your minor is Shutting Up. The curriculum is divided into three mandatory departments.

Department 1: The Shop Class (Hard Skills / Doing)

Course Title: How to Not Be Useless 101.

This is the physical curriculum. It is the antidote to ideation. In this department, we deal exclusively with objects, not feelings, and the only metric for success is whether the thing actually works.

The Syllabus: Practical Utility

1. **The Hammer, The Saw, & The Siphon:** A Gen X Trinity. This module covers the essential toolkit: how to drive a nail straight, how to cut wood square, and the non-negotiable science of siphoning gas without poisoning yourself. This is the difference between shelter and exposure.

2. **Basic Fucking Mechanics:** Spark Plugs, Oil, and Why That Check Engine Light Used to Matter. Forget the dashboard computer. We are focused on the holy trinity of combustion. You will learn how to change oil, identify a seized piston, and fix a broken pull-cord. We are no longer reliant on the magic box mentality; you must understand the basic, dirty, internal mechanics of everything that goes vroom.

3. **Poop Goes Downhill:** A Primer on Basic Plumbing and Sanitation. This is the single most important lesson in public health. You will learn how to build a simple latrine system, how to secure water lines, and why your compound is two days away from an outbreak of cholera if you ignore the septic field. This is the janitor's path to autonomy.

4. **Mending 100:** You Will Learn to Sew a Goddamn Button. Yes, you. We reject the consumer culture of disposal. A tear does not mean abandonment. You will learn to mend a rip, patch a hole, and secure a button. Durability is survival.

The Gen X Lesson (The Grade)

We are not grading on a curve. We are grading on survival.

The old world allowed you to say, "That's not my job," or, "I don't know how." Those answers are now classified as lethally stupid.

The new mandate is simple:

1. The answer to "I don't know how" is: "Then fucking learn."

2. The answer to "That's not my job" is: "It is now."

Your performance review is whether or not you lived through the night. Nothing else matters.

Department 2: The Home Ec (Soft Skills / Surviving)

Course Title: How to Not Starve 201.

This is the sustenance curriculum. It is the antidote to passion-aligned projects. You don't align with food; you eat it. This department focuses on the mental resilience and forgotten skills necessary to maintain a caloric surplus without access to an Amazon Prime account.

The Syllabus: Sustenance and Self-Care

1. **The Latchkey Kid's Challenge:** How to Survive a 3-Day Weekend with No Adults, No Internet, and One Frozen Pizza. (The required reading.) This module is the synthesis of our childhood trauma. It teaches students how to stretch limited, pathetic resources over maximum time, using creativity and low expectations. The primary lesson: boredom and hunger are not emergencies; they are solvable problems.

2. **Canning, Pickling, & Preserving:** Or, How to Not Get Scurvy. We shift the focus from consumerism to agriculture. You will learn the difference between eating a potato now and saving it for winter. This is the practical science of longevity. You will learn the most critical skill: deferring gratification for survival.

3. **First Aid 202:** It's Just a Scrape. Rub Some Dirt on It. (Critiquing the "need an ER for a papercut" mindset). This module reverses the damage done by the over-careful generation. You will learn to recognize the difference between a minor injury (which you handle with a piece of cloth and a shot of whiskey) and a fatal one (where you call for help). It re-establishes radical self-reliance for minor injuries, freeing up limited medical supplies for genuine triage.

153

4. **The Leftover Thesis:** How to Make Dinner out of Ketchup Packets, One Egg, and a Wish. This is the Iron Chef module. You learn resourcefulness. You learn that expired is a guideline, not a law. You learn that a meal is a functional assembly of calories, not a carefully balanced plate of nutrition.

The goal of this department is to make the survivor food-secure and medically stable enough to not require constant, annoying intervention from the Gen X functionalists.

Department 3: The Recess (Mental Skills / Coping)

Course Title: How to Be Bored 301 (And Not Have a Meltdown).

This is, counterintuitively, the most important department. You can fix the generator and mend the clothes, but if your mind breaks, you invite the horde inside. This is the antidote to the attention economy. We are teaching you the lost art of doing fucking nothing.

The Syllabus: The Lost Art of Doing Nothing

1. **The Staring at the Ceiling Seminar (45 minutes. Mandatory):** This is the core meditation technique of the Gen X experience. There is no talking. There is no content. There is no phone (it is locked away). You just think. We are re-introducing you to your own head. The goal is not to clear your mind; the goal is to confront the terrifying silence of your own thoughts and realize that you are not dependent on external stimuli for existence.

2. **The Analog Lab:** We give you the resources of a 1980s rainy afternoon: a book (paper, with pages), a deck of cards, a notebook and a pen, and maybe a guitar with two strings. Now, entertain yourself. We'll be back in three hours. You must learn to generate your own narrative, not consume one. Boredom is the engine of creativity; you will either solve a complex problem or write a terrible poem. Both are productive.

3. **The Walk Practicum (Mandatory, Alone):** You are instructed to go outside the safe zone and patrol the inner perimeter. Alone. You do not document it. You do not wear

headphones. You just...walk. You listen. You observe. You come back when you're done. This teaches you to manage solitude, to appreciate the silence, and to convert your energy into a functional output (patrol) rather than emotional noise.

The Gen X Lesson (The Power of Boredom)

We are re-introducing you to the single most powerful Gen X tool of all: boredom. Boredom is not a void; it is a forge.

Boredom is where resilience, creativity, and problem-solving are born. We were raised by boredom. It forced us to use our brains to survive those long, empty afternoons.

It's time you were, too.

The Graduation

The new re-education isn't a four-year program. It's a life program. It's constant. The campus is the compound, and the lessons are delivered by the immutable laws of physics and biology.

But there must be a final exam.

The test is simple. We leave you alone for a weekend (just like our parents did). We leave you with the inventory, the maintenance schedule, and the locked gate.

When we come back, we check the results:

1. Is the compound not on fire?

2. Have you not starved?

3. Are you not currently in a processing circle about the trauma of being alone?

If the answer to all three is yes, you graduate.

We're not creating scholars. We're not creating activists. We're not creating influencers. We're creating functional, fucking adults. We're creating more of us. Not because we want to (God, no), but because someone has to.

And once you have a compound full of functional, non-annoying adults, you run into the final, ultimate Gen X problem. You've built a system that works. It's competent. It's stable. It's...boring.

Which means...you're stuck running it. Unless...unless you can figure out how to not be the new Boomer.

Chapter 18

Don't Become the New Boomer: A Self-Awareness Check

The Gray Water Incident

It's been a year since the WJDBAA Doctrine took effect. And the truth is, it works. The generator hums, the walls are solid, and the most dramatic event of the week was a heated debate over whether to plant carrots or potatoes. It's quiet. It's functional. You are, for the first time in your entire life, in charge of something that isn't a total disaster.

The quiet, naturally, is dangerous.

You're taking stock of the water filtration system, admiring your own simple, elegant pipework. One of the kids—Leo, a Gen Zer you personally trained in basic engineering—approaches you.

"Hey," Leo says, a little nervous. "So, I was looking at the cistern schematic...the one you drew..."

(...Oh god, what now?) is your immediate, internal monologue.

"It's really smart," Leo continues. "But I was thinking...if we re-route this one pipe, we can use all the gray water from the sinks to irrigate the lower garden beds. It would be about 20% more water efficient."

And you feel it. The immediate, hot, defensive anger.

The Boomer gut reaction is automatic:

"What?"

"Kid, that system works. It works fine."

"I built that system. I know how it works. You mess with one pipe, the whole thing could go down. It's risky."

"We're lucky to have any water. Why are you trying to change things? Why can't you just follow the plan that works?"

You stop. You catch your breath. And the realization hits you with the sickening force of a sudden stop. You just heard yourself. You just sounded exactly like your dad when you tried to show him how the new (1992) remote control worked. You just sounded like Bob from the HOA.

The final, hardest boss in the apocalypse isn't a king zombie. It's not the Boomer with the bullhorn. It's the inner boomer.

It's the part of us that finally got the world running our way...and is fucking terrified to let anyone else touch it. This is the test. Don't fuck it up.

The Philosophy - Boomerism as a Disease of Success

The moment you heard your own voice demand, "Why are you trying to change things?" you witnessed the genesis of the enemy within.

Boomerism isn't an age. It's a symptom of success. It's the rigidity that sets in when your way (which was genuinely better) becomes the only way. It's the exact, calcified defense mechanism we've spent our entire lives rolling our eyes at.

This is how the boomer playbook infects the Gen X mind:

- **The Good Old Days Fallacy:** We're this close to sounding like them. "You kids have it easy! You didn't see what it was like at the fall! We had to fight for this compound!" We start glorifying our own struggle and dismissing theirs—as if the work Leo is doing now isn't just as difficult as the triage we did then. We mistake competence for innate superiority.
- **Weaponized Competence:** We are competent. We did fix the generator. We are now using this undeniable fact as a weapon to shut down all new ideas. "Look, I built it. I know better. End of discussion." The moment our knowledge becomes an excuse for deafness, we've failed. Knowledge should be a platform for innovation, not a picket fence against change.
- **The Entitlement Echo:** We hated Boomers for feeling entitled to the world they inherited. We are now in mortal danger of feeling entitled to run this new world, simply because we saved it. We begin to believe that our suffering earned us permanent, unquestionable authority. This is the cardinal sin of the old regime, and it's how we transform from fixer to manager.
- **The Deafness:** This is the most dangerous element. The refusal to listen. Dismissing new ideas before hearing them. Assuming we know best, 100% of the time. Leo suggested a

20% efficiency increase. Our internal Boomer didn't hear "20% efficiency"; it heard "threat to my authority."

The Gen X Self-Correction must be immediate.

We are the forgotten middle child. Our entire identity was forged in not being the special Boomer or the special Millennial. The moment we start thinking we're special—that our way is the only way—we've lost. We've become the exact thing we defined ourselves against. The Inner Boomer must be identified, mocked, and retired to the back benches immediately.

The How-To - The Gen X Boomer Vaccine (A 4-Step Checklist)

This is the self-awareness imperative. You are not the boss. You are the chief janitor. Here's how to stay that way by preventing the Inner Boomer from seizing control of the compound.

Step 1: Shut Up and Listen (The 48-Hour Rule).

The Inner Boomer's first instinct is the immediate, dismissive "No." This is the voice of rigidity, fear, and ego. You must muzzle that voice.

The Rule: When a kid (like Leo) brings you a new idea, your gut screams 'No.' Your training must be silence. You are not allowed to give a final no for 48 hours.

The How-To: Instead of "No," you ask one question: "Show me." Or "Prove it on a small scale." Or "Draw it." You force them to back up their idea with competence, which separates the good ideas from the Blaze-level stupid ones.

You're not just testing them; you are forcing yourself to listen and engage with the idea as a technical challenge, not a personal slight. You redirect the conversation from "Why are you bothering me?" to "What are the specs?"

The Reason: This isn't their test. It's yours. You're testing your own ability to not be a rigid asshole. If you can successfully overcome your innate defensive impulse and listen to a twenty-year-old suggest an improvement on your system, you pass the test. You've proven you're still a fixer, not a manager.

160

Step 2: Distinguish Stupid from New (The Gen X Triage).

The 48-Hour Rule is only the first layer of defense. You must now distinguish between two very different categories of suggestion: stupid (the Boomer/Blaze level) and new (the Leo level). Your job is not to say "yes" to everything; your job is to triage the risk.

The Rule: Not all new ideas are good. Our job is to triage the consequence, not the intention. This isn't Boomer rigidity; this is Gen X rationality.

The How-To: When presented with the idea, you ask two ruthless questions that prioritize survival over novelty:

1. What's the Risk? (The Failure Cost): If this fails, do we all die? If the answer is yes, or if it costs irreversible resources (like the last of the antibiotics), the idea is stupid. (Verdict: no.)
2. What's the Reward? (The Potential Gain): If it works, is it actually better? Does it make us more efficient, quieter, or safer? If the gain is negligible (like improving the aesthetic), it's also stupid. (Verdict: no.)

The Reason (Applying the Logic):

Leo's Gray Water Idea.

- Risk? Low. He's only tapping one pipe. The main cistern remains secure. If it fails, we lose some sink water, not drinking water.
- Reward? High. 20% more water efficiency.
- Verdict: Let him fucking try.

Aiden's (Millennial) Idea: "Let's see if zombies can be reasoned with by playing them peaceful folk music."

- Risk? High. You get eaten.
- Reward? Low. They can't be reasoned with.
- Verdict: No. And you're on latrine duty.

This process ensures that your authority is used not as a blanket of oppression, but as a surgical instrument of risk management. You prevent the catastrophic failures while promoting the useful innovations.

Step 3: Promote the Plumber (Delegate Real Authority).

You can't be the Chief Plumber forever. The whole point of the Re-Education curriculum was to create competent, functional adults—so use them. This is the only way you achieve your ultimate goal: the quiet couch.

The Rule: You cannot be the chief plumber forever. The moment you've trained a new plumber...you give them the fucking plumbing.

The How-To: This is the hardest part because it requires trust. It means letting them make a mistake. It means not supervising by standing over their shoulder, sighing heavily.

You delegate authority, not just tasks. You give them the keys to the generator room. You hand over the schematics (even your secret ones, the ones with the extra notations and grease stains). You actively work to make yourself obsolete.

The Reason: A Boomer delegates tasks ("Go fetch that pipe"). A Gen X-er must delegate authority ("You are now responsible for the entire plumbing system").

The Boomer delegates because they want to control the outcome while avoiding the work. The Gen X-er delegates because they want the work to be done correctly by the person who is currently focused on it. This is the only way you finally get to go sit on that couch. You transition from being the indispensable wrench to the semi-retired consultant—and the price of your consultation is peace and quiet.

Step 4: Remember Your First Mixtape (Embrace Their Shit).

This is the ultimate test of humility and the antidote to the inner Boomer's cultural arrogance.

The Rule: We hated when Boomers shit on our music ("That's just noise!"). We hated when they shit on our clothes. We hated when they shit on our slang. Do. Not. Do. This.

The How-To: When the kids start their own culture in the compound—their own (terrible) music, their own (stupid) art, their own (baffling) slang—you leave it the fuck alone. It's not for you. That's the point.

162

You must allow for the creation of new, organic forms of non-essential human activity. If Leo starts a band that sounds like three guys arguing over a broken synthesizer, you don't criticize the melody. You nod, thank him for his efficiency in using scrap metal, and walk away.

The Reason: Their culture is the proof that your system is working. It's the ultimate win. The compound is so safe and so functional that they have the luxury of being kids. They have the security to experiment, be bored, and be annoying without lethal consequence.

You did that. You built the walls and fixed the pipes that created this space. Now, shut up and let them enjoy it. Your job is not to curate their existence. Your job is to ensure their existence. The ultimate Gen X victory is the sound of music you hate being played through a speaker you fixed.

The Fade, Not the Reign

The final contrast is the most important.

The Boomer reigns. They lecture. They demand respect. They stay in charge until they're dragged out, clinging to the power they feel they've earned. They die on the throne, convinced of their own indispensability.

The Gen X path is the opposite: A Gen Xer must fade. Our entire life was a masterclass in fading—into the background, into our music, into our own heads. This is the final skill.

The new Goal is not to become the new kings. Our job was to be the technicians and the architects of the system. Now, our job is to be the consultants. We are the grizzled mentors in the back, cleaning a rifle, who only speak up when someone is seconds away from doing something lethally stupid.

The ultimate Gen X win is not to be in charge. It's to build a system so good and train a generation so competent that we are no longer fucking needed.

This transition, this intentional obsolescence, is the only way to retire.

And that...that is the true Gen X utopia. It's not a place. It's a state of being. It's the absence of responsibility. It's the absence of drama. It's finally...finally...achieving the one thing we've always wanted: a quiet fucking couch.

Chapter 19
Defining Success (It Probably Involves a Quiet Couch and a Locked Gate)

The Meeting That Didn't Happen

You made it. You successfully achieved the fade. You walk across the compound, and the air itself feels lightened, like someone finally fixed the low-grade hum of anxiety that permeated the old world. It's quiet. Not scared quiet, but functional quiet.

You see a notice tacked to the community board: "10 AM: Compound Infrastructure & Resource Meeting."

Instinct takes over. Your stomach clenches. A meeting. The primal terror of the Gen X experience. A meeting about infrastructure. You're already bracing for the committee-forming, the ideation-session, and the performative apologies.

You trudge to the mess hall at 10:01 AM, lukewarm coffee in hand, ready for the pain. The hall is empty.

...Except for Leo, the plumbing apprentice, who is quietly sweeping up spilled grain.

The dialogue begins with the confusion of a man who has missed a major crisis.

"Where is...it?" you ask.

Leo looks up, genuinely confused. "What?"

"The...meeting?"

Leo shrugs. "Oh. Yeah, we canceled that. I ran the new gray-water numbers last night, and Skye's team already finished the pipe retrofit. We're saving 20% water. It's...done. Seemed stupid to have a meeting about something that's finished."

He just...goes back to sweeping.

You stand there, stunned, the mug of coffee trembling in your hand. The system worked. The kids handled it. The meeting was pre-emptively identified as bullshit and canceled. You are not needed.

This...this is it. This is the dream. This is the win.

For our entire lives, we were fed two definitions of success—the Boomer reign and the Millennial brand. Both were traps. The real Gen X utopia was never about power or fame. It was about this: a

166

quiet morning, a working system, and the glorious, profound, beautiful absence of a fucking meeting.

The Philosophy - Deconstructing the Pyramid Scheme of Bullshit

The dream we were sold in the old world was a lie. It was a pyramid scheme of bullshit designed to prop up two generations of drama while the middle was bled dry.

We have to understand the architecture of that scheme to appreciate why the current silence is the victory.

The Boomer Dream (The Reign): Their success was the corner office. A title. Power. They wanted to be the boss, make the rules, and lecture everyone.

The cost? They could never rest. They had to be the boss, 24/7. They had to attend every meeting, manage every underling, and defend their position from rivals. Their "success" was a prison of their own ego. They were the shark that had to keep swimming or die.

The Millennial/Gen Z Dream (The Brand): Their success was the personal brand. Influence. Validation. A passion that was also their job. They wanted to be known, seen, and affirmed by their invisible audience.

The Cost? They could never be off. Their success was a 24/7 performance for an invisible audience. They had to document the journey, process the trauma, and prove their worth daily. Their success was a prison of attention.

The Gen X Trap: And us? We were the mediocre cogs holding both of their broken systems together. We did the work for the Boomer's reign and provided the stability for the Millennial/Gen Z performance. We were the engine...and the janitors. We were the indispensable middle layer that paid for the whole ridiculous structure.

The Great Reversal: Then, the zombies ate the pyramid.

The CEOs and influencers were the first to go because they were too busy defending their turf or filming their exit to notice the threat. All that brand synergy and corporate leadership meant nothing when the power grid failed.

167

The pyramid shattered. All that's left is the ground floor.

And it's so. fucking. quiet. The chaos is gone, replaced by the simple, beautiful logic of functionality. This is why the meeting that didn't happen is the greatest achievement of the new world.

The New Gen X Manifesto of Success (The 4 Pillars of The Couch)

This is the new dream. It's not a *place*; it's a state of being. It is the Philosophy of the Quiet Couch.

Pillar 1: The Hum (Success is Functional).

The old world defined success by what you acquired—a Rolex, a sports car, a blue checkmark. The new definition of success is based on what functions.

The Argument: The new status symbol isn't a Rolex or a blue checkmark. It's the hum.

The How-To: To understand this, you must pause. Stand in the middle of the compound and listen. What do you hear?

The low, steady hum of the generator.

The gentle gurgle of clean water moving through the pipes.

The definitive click of a locked gate.

What you don't hear is: shouting, panic, alarms, or whining.

Old world success was drama. Gen X success is the profound lack of it. It's the sound of competence. It's the sound of 'Whatever, it just works.' The fact that the generator has become so reliable that you tune it out—that's the ultimate indicator of prosperity. It's boring, and it's beautiful.

Pillar 2: The Good Shit (Success is Analog & Real).

The old world was drowning in crap. Content. Swag. Fast-fashion. An entire economy built on cheap, disposable plastic and ephemeral digital noise. We're done with crap. The new definition of success is quality.

The Argument: Success isn't measured by volume. It's measured by durability and sensory pleasure. It is the curation of what doesn't suck.

168

The How-To: It's not about having all the coffee. It's about having one cup of real fucking coffee (the title drop) that you ground yourself from a single, scavenged bag of beans. It's not an algorithm-fed playlist; it's your copy of 'Violator' on the one working turntable (the title drop) that still sounds crisp because you maintained the belt.

It's one good pair of boots that lasts. It's one solid chair. The items are tangible, they are functional, and they produce a genuine, non-performative pleasure.

And here's the key: We still have them because we maintained them. While the Millennial treated their phone like a disposable tissue and the Boomer treated their car like a magic carpet that the dealership fixed, we oiled the leather. We cleaned the needle. We accepted that 'owning' something means taking care of it. That's why our boots are dry and theirs are rotting.

We reject the idea that more is better. Success isn't abundance; it's the efficient, functional quality of the essential. The ultimate joy is the feel of a worn, quality item that you know how to fix, used in silence.

Pillar 3: The My Time Doctrine (Success is Autonomy).

In the old world, the ultimate luxury was money. It bought you things. The ultimate luxury in the new world is uninterrupted fucking time.

The Argument: Time is the most precious, non-renewable resource. Success is defined by the absolute control you have over your own time—and that control is earned through the competence of others.

The How-To: This is the true meaning of the quiet couch. It is the direct result of passing the test in Chapter 18.

Because you trained Leo. Because you delegated the authority. Because the system is functional, you can now sit on that couch for three straight hours with a book. And nobody...fucking...bothers you.

That, right there, is the corner office. That is fuck you money. It is the absolute control over your own time—time you didn't have to spend arguing with Bob or fixing something that was obviously preventable. You have successfully outsourced all the drama. This autonomy is the highest form of wealth.

Pillar 4: The Full Sentence No (Success is Voluntary).

This is the glorious final result of the Gen X experience. The ultimate power is not the power to do. It's the power to NOT do. It's the end of mandatory fun.

The Argument: Success is when your presence is optional. It is the non-negotiable freedom of choice, earned through years of being involuntarily trapped in group activities.

The How-To: Remember the meeting that didn't happen? That's the goal. Your success is when you are no longer required at the planning session or the community circle.

It's when "No" is a complete sentence.

Chad approaches: "Are you coming to the new harvest strategy meeting?"

You respond: "No."

And that's it. No excuse. No passive-aggressive sigh. No lengthy explanation about the gray water project. Just..."No."

Watch his face. He freezes. He is waiting for the because...He is waiting for the excuse he can negotiate with, or the apology he can validate. When it doesn't come, his operating system crashes. He nods, confused, and walks away. You didn't just win the argument; you deleted the argument.

The Reason: Because the system works. You've earned 'No.' You created a world where your presence is no longer required for basic functionality. You are free. The reward for competence is the ability to decline participation in idiocy. You are now a voluntary participant in the future you built.

The Retirement We Were Never Going to Get

Let's be brutally honest. We were never going to get to retire in the old world.

We were the sandwich generation", destined to spend our prime earning years cleaning up messes. We were designed to prop up the Boomers' broken social system (healthcare, pensions, housing

170

market) and fund the Millennials' self-discovery (student loans, endless job hopping), all while working ourselves to death. The reward was a heart attack at 62 and a retirement spent managing our aging parents and our twenty-something kids.

The apocalypse was our retirement party.

It was the market correction we were all waiting for. It burned down the pyramid of bullshit and smashed the sandwich. It excused us from all future meetings. We were freed not by wealth, but by total systemic collapse.

The Gen X dream was always just peace. A quiet place. A locked gate. A working generator. A good stereo. And not one single fucking person asking you, "Hey, you got a minute?"

The Boomer dream was power. The Millennial/Gen Z dream was fame. The Gen X dream was autonomy. And here we are. It took the end of the world, but we won.

We built it. It works.

...So now what? We're done. Which means...it's finally time to do what we've been training our entire lives to do. It's time to disappear.

Chapter 20
Fade to Black: We Built It. It Works. We're Going to Bed.

The Keys on the Hook

It's been months since the constitutional convention that wasn't. The compound is, blessedly, boring. The crops are in. The walls are secure. The kids—Leo, Skye, Aiden—are competent. They run the perimeter checks, they manage the rotation, and they even clean the water filters without being told.

You've achieved the ultimate goal: The compound no longer needs you to function.

The inciting incident is subtle. You're not packing armor or extra ammo. You're packing a small duffel bag. A thermos (of the good coffee). A book you've been meaning to read for fifteen years. A fresh set of batteries for your Walkman.

Leo, the now-chief plumber, finds you in your quarters. He sees the bag and his eyes go wide with residual, Millennial-era panic.

"Hey. Uh...you're...packing. Is...is something wrong?" he asks, his voice tight. "Did I miss a perimeter breach?"

"Wrong? No," you say, zipping the bag. "Everything's right. The generator's humming. The water's clean. The gate's locked."

"So...where are you going? You're...you're not...leaving...are you?"

You stop, looking him straight in the eye. "Nope. I'm retiring."

The clincher is the final, physical act of delegation. You walk with him to the main operations board. You take the master set of keys—the ones for the generator shed, the armory, the main gate—and you hang them on a central, empty hook.

Leo stares at the keys, his panic palpable. "But...who's in charge?"

You point to him, then around the room. "You are. He is. She is. Whoever's on shift. The system is in charge. You know the system."

"But...what if...what if I mess up?"

You give him the gentlest Gen X shrug possible. "You will. Then you'll fix it. Then you'll learn. It's your shift."

And then you walk out. Not out of the compound. You walk to that small, repaired lookout post on the far edge of the perimeter. The one with the good chimney and the comfortable-looking chair on

174

the porch. This is the fade to black. It's not an abandonment. It's the final promotion. We've finally achieved the obsolescence we've been working for. The job is done. We're going to bed.

The Philosophy - The Anti-Legacy as the Ultimate Legacy

Every other generation is obsessed with their legacy. It's the disease of the main character, the constant, desperate need to be remembered.

The Boomer legacy is physical and rigid: a plaque, a statue, or a building with their name on it. They want to be the founder. Their retirement is just another stage for them to lecture from, ensuring they remain the center of the narrative.

The Millennial legacy is performative and narrative: a documentary about their journey, a community art project honoring their struggle. They need their story to be told and affirmed. Their retirement is a curated Instagram post.

The Gen X legacy (the fade) is the opposite. We hate all of that. We never wanted the spotlight. Our entire identity was forged in the shadows of the Boomers' spotlight. The reward for saving the world isn't a parade. The reward is no longer having to fucking save it.

Our true legacy is the hum. It's the working generator they don't know how to fix but don't have to worry about. It's the clean water they don't know how to purify but get to drink. Our legacy is a self-sustaining system that makes us forgotten.

We want to be forgotten. Forgotten means it's working.

This isn't the hero's journey. It's the technician's journey. We're not the hero who gets the medal. We're the grizzled detective who solved the case, and while the mayor is giving a speech to the press, we're already in our car, lighting a cigarette, and driving away.

Credits roll. Fade to black.

The How-To - The Note Left on the Fridge (Final Instructions for the New World)

This is the hand-off. This is the true new constitution. It's the user's manual for the compound we're leaving on the table with the keys. This is the simple set of rules for the new generation to keep the peace we earned.

Rule 1: Don't Call Us. (Unless It's Really on Fire.)

This is the title drop rule. It is the core of the new social contract: We are retired, and our time is sacred.

The Argument: We are not your help desk. We are not your managers. You are re-educated. You are competent. You know the Five-Minute Crisis Protocol. Your panic is not our problem. Our retirement is our priority.

The How-To: Before you dare walk across that compound to ask a quick question, you must try to solve it three fucking times yourself. That's the barrier to entry. If you haven't exhausted your own resources and the resources of your competent shift partners, the answer is automatically no.

The Fine Print: The only exception is the Fire & 10 rule. If the problem involves active flames AND more than 10 zombies, you have permission to knock. Once. Otherwise, it's your shift. Your failure to prepare does not constitute an emergency on our part.

Rule 2: Don't Fuck With the Stereo.

This rule is the Don't Become the New Boomer rule, in reverse. It is the core cultural boundary you are establishing.

The Argument: We built this world. We let you live in it. We let you run it. But that's our record collection. That's our (terrible) '90s music. You do not get to re-curate it.

The How-To (The Metaphor): This isn't just about the music—it's a metaphor for the foundation of the compound. It means respect the fucking source code.

You can innovate, but you do not get to break the foundation just because it feels traditional or problematic.

The compound is built on:

1. Function over feelings.

2. Competence over consensus.

3. Whatever, just don't be an asshole.

You want to change the lighting system? Fine. You want to change the core operating principles that ensure our survival? You don't. You are free to create a new culture that exists on top of the structure we built, but you don't get to mess with the engine.

Rule 3: Don't Form a Fucking Committee.

This is the original sin. This is the one thing that will make us come back. And we will be pissed.

The Argument: The committee is the engine of bullshit and stagnation. It is the enemy of action. It's the mechanism that destroyed the old world's ability to respond to a crisis.

The How-To: You must recognize the progression of failure, and you must stop it at stage 1:

1. The moment you have a meeting to plan a future meeting...you have failed.

2. The moment you form a sub-committee to generate a report...you have failed.

3. The moment you circle back on ideation...you are the new Boomer, and you are the new enemy.

You must remember the core principle of the new government: Just do the fucking work. If you see a problem, fix it. If you can't fix it, delegate authority to the person who can. Do not delegate the decision to a group of people who are not currently focused on the problem.

Rule 4: Leave Us Some Coffee.

This is the articulation of the new economy and the consultant fee for our earned silence.

The Argument: We're not dead. We're consultants. We're the grizzled mentors on the hill. We still exist. But our time is ours. It's not free.

The How-To (The New Economy): This is the price for our wisdom (when you actually need it, see Rule 1). You handle the drama. You handle the bullshit. You handle the daily grind. And in exchange, you tithe to the retired Gen Xers.

The tithe must be paid in: coffee, ammunition, and silence.

You leave the good shit on our porch—the fresh filters, the sharpest ammo, the best scavenged books. And we, in turn, will continue to not meddle in your affairs.

It's the perfect Gen X social contract.' We keep the existential chaos at bay for you, and you keep the quiet couch stocked for us. We are no longer required to be present, but we are required to be paid. In peace.

The Hum. The Couch. The Silence.

The final scene is set. You are on that porch, the retirement cabin'on the far edge of the compound. It's dusk.

The Senses: The proof of peace. You can hear it. It's the hum— the steady, boring, beautiful thrum of the generator you fixed a year ago. It's the sound of a functional, living compound: distant laughter, the soft clank of a hammer (someone is building, not fighting). Crucially, what you don't hear is: screaming, alarms, or, God forbid, meetings.

You look down at the compound. You see the kids—Leo, Skye, and the others—closing the main gate for the night. They do not even look at you. They don't need to. They got this.

The Final Summary:

The Cost of Peace. For decades, we were the forgotten middle child". We were the sandwich generation, stuck cleaning up the Boomers' messes and managing the Millennials' feelings. We were the engine nobody saw, the janitors nobody thanked. We didn't want the dream. We just wanted out.

And here we are. It took the end of the fucking world, but we're finally out. We're forgotten again. But this time...it's on our own terms. It's not neglect; it's respect. It's the retirement we were never going to get.